Black Marxism

Black Marxism

A Marxist Critique

by AUGUST H. NIMTZ

MONTHLY REVIEW PRESS
New York

Library of Congress Cataloging-in-Publication data
available from the publisher.

ISBN 978-168590-173-8 paper
ISBN 978-168590-174-5 cloth

Typeset in Arno Pro

MONTHLY REVIEW PRESS | NEW YORK
www.monthlyreview.org

5 4 3 2 1

Contents

Preface | 7

1 Fortuitious Biography as Prelude | 15
2 *Black Marxism*: The First In-Depth Review | 34
3 The Eurocentric Marx and Engels and Other Related Myths | 59
4 Marx on Race: What the Critics Get Wrong | 81
5 Revisiting *Black Marxism* Four Decades Later: Bringing Marx into the Class-versus-Race Debate | 123

Bibliography | 170
Notes | 177
Index | 201

To radicalizing youth everywhere
in quest of the real Marx.

Preface

THIS COLLECTION INTENDS TO BE an intervention into a discussion and debate initiated with the publication in 1983 of *Black Marxism: The Making of the Black Radical Tradition*—a potentially consequential debate in the Trump era—about the ever-present and still unresolved "class-versus-race" question. Let's begin with some historical background.

"Cedric Robinson's *Black Marxism,*" Cornel West wrote in the September 1988 issue of *Monthly Review,* "is the most significant challenge to American Marxist and black left thought and practice since Harold Cruse's *The Crisis of the Negro Intellectual* (1967). Unfortunately, Robinson's book has not yet received the kind of critical attention it deserves. Though published in 1983, the book has already fallen through the cracks—a fate to be avoided if at all possible. . . . Robinson's book is a towering achievement. There is simply nothing like it in the history of black radical thought."[1]

Contrary to West's claim about the book not having gotten "the kind of critical attention it deserves," three years earlier the vanguard London-based *Journal of African Marxists* (*JAM*) had done just that.[2] It published the 7,000-word critical review—almost 5,000 more words than West's—that it had solicited from me.

Historian Robin D. G. Kelley, twelve years later, also noted that mainstream journals ignored *Black Marxism*. In Kelley's foreword to the 2000 republication of the book, the "few reviews [*Black Marxism*] did receive, were [from] left-leaning publications or very specialized journals, and the only substantial review essays that dealt with the book at length were written by Cornel West and the radical Black philosopher Leonard Harris, with both published several years after the book appeared."[3] Kelley's claim about "the only substantial review essays" is belied by the review published in the *Journal of African Marxists.*

I'd mostly forgotten about my essay until 2017, when Kelley's renewed praise for *Black Marxism* in the *Boston Review* brought new attention to Robinson's book. As Kelley wrote, "*Black Marxism* was largely ignored for two decades, until its return to print in 2000 generated renewed interest." That neglect surely had nothing to do with my unsparing—as readers will see—1984 critique of the book, its first serious review, except maybe for a small group of *JAM*-connected readers. An extensive Google Scholar search turned up only one citation for my review, a republished Portuguese version in Brazil in 2021.[4] But given West's effusive 1988 endorsement, in *Monthly Review,* a venue more accessible than *JAM,* it remains a mystery why the book was "largely ignored for two decades" after its original publication in 1983.

In the foreword to the book's republication in 2021, Kelley wrote: "When the London-based Zed Press published *Black Marxism* in 1983, few could have predicted the impact it would have on political theory, political economy, historical analysis, Black Studies, Marxist studies, or our general understanding of the rise of the modern world. It appeared with little fanfare. For years it was treated as a curiosity, grossly misunderstood or simply ignored."[5] Again, not so in the case of the London-based *JAM*. Only in hindsight, four decades later, might there be an explanation for that neglect. It's what my critique of *Black Marxism* noted at the very end and what West and Kelley failed to see in their readings and glowing opinions about the book—Robinson's apparent unawareness of what was taking place in the real world of politics in 1983 and, hence, the mostly silent response to the book.

I discovered that I had misplaced my copy of my review, and only through interlibrary loan did I retrieve one. Eventually I found the copy *JAM* had sent to me, along with, as the reader will learn, important correspondence long forgotten. Given all the attention *Black Marxism* was getting with its republication in 2021, I tried, unsuccessfully, to convince various publications I thought would be interested in reprinting it. Only in Brazil, as noted above, did I find one, and then later, the website *Academia*.[6] Many thanks to Jared Ball's "Black Power Media" web program for granting me an interview in 2023, which garnered some newfound interest in my 1985 review.[7]

I'm forever indebted to Michael Yates and the editorial team at *Monthly Review*—Susie Day especially for her careful eyes and truly thought-provoking questions—for not only republishing the 1985 review here, but also for including two subsequent publications to accompany it—along with an original concluding essay. Most important, I'm grateful to have been urged to think about how to bring all those earlier publications and the new essay into a coherent whole. Special thanks to the anonymous reader who pointed out the three different editions of Robinson's book. Also, to Sanna Nimtz Towns and Joseph Towns IV for helping me to clarify the purpose of this Preface.

This collection is the product of a more than four-decades-long engagement with Karl Marx and Frederick Engels's communist project. My not-so-hidden agenda has been to liberate Marx from the embrace of philosophers and theorists—sometimes well-meaning—and to bring him back into the world of politics that he consciously chose to join around 1843. *Marx and Engels: Their Contribution to the Democratic Breakthrough*, in 2000, was my first book, followed three years later by my *Marx, Tocqueville, and Race in America*. A decade and a half later, in 2019, after engaging Lenin, I wrote *Marxism versus Liberalism*; then, most recently, with Kyle Edwards, published *The Communist and the Revolutionary Liberal in the Second American Revolution: Comparing Karl Marx and Frederick Douglass in Real-Time*.[8]

This book begins with an "about the author" essay, necessary for understanding why the first in-depth review of *Black Marxism* was not, unlike the subsequent accolades that greeted the book, impressed with its claims, in fact deeply critical. We're all, as Marx would have explained, products of circumstances over which we have no control. Chapter 1 thus allows for a comparison with Robinson's biography, a fellow African American and age cohort, that likely accounts for two different political trajectories and, thus, readings of and conclusions about real world politics in that epoch.[9]

Chapter 2, my 1985 critique of Robinson's book, begins with an introduction that explains the circumstances of its writing and publication. With historical perspective, the introduction highlights what I argue to be the article's enduring significance—awareness, unlike *Black Marxism*, of real-time politics. Chapter 3, a 2002 essay that addresses Marx's alleged Eurocentrism—a central charge in Robinson's narrative—elaborates on the tidbits of counterfactuals supplied in the 1985 review. The chapter's introduction explains the reason for the more informed response to Robinson's charge than was possible seventeen years earlier. Chapter 4, "Marx on Race: What the Critics Get Wrong," is a

2024 essay that defends Marx and Engels from five recent critics, four of whom rely on Robinson for authority to do so.

Last, chapter 5, "Revisiting *Black Marxism* Four Decades Later: Bringing Marx into the Class-versus-Race Debate," is informed by my most recent dive into Marx's project. Comparing Karl Marx and Frederick Douglass on how they responded to the Second American Revolution, the U.S. Civil War, revealed a Marx more aware of the race question than I knew when I wrote my 1985 review and is contrary to what Robinson and his fans allege about Marx on the question.[10] What happens, the Marx-Douglass book asks, when we put Marx up against the best that the "Black radical tradition" has to offer in real-time politics?[11] The implication of those findings for today's politics, "What is to be done?," is the subject of the chapter's second part.

In his foreword to the 2000 edition of *Black Marxism*, Kelley saw the need to provide political context for Robinson's book, both in time and space. But, as I wrote in 1985, that's the deficit that makes *Black Marxism* so problematic, the absence of attention to what was underway in the actual political world, tellingly unlike, I contend, the authentic Marxist project. Revisiting *Black Marxism* reveals a political liability that looms even larger today, which distinguishes my critique from other recent and critical ones. Those of us, fortunately still alive, who lived through and know about that moment in which Robinson wrote his book—and to which he was seemingly oblivious—are obligated to say so.

Kelley, twenty years my junior, wrote in his 2000 foreword that, "without a trace of hyperbole," Robinson's book "changed my life."[12] One can only speculate on what impact, if any, my 1985 critique of *Black Marxism* might have had on the course of the young graduate student, had he by chance read it as well. But only, to repeat, at the very end of my review did I point to what is clearer today—the failure of Robinson to address the actuality and "living reality" of world politics. Thus, Kelley, had he seen my review in real time, could have missed my main—and crucial— point.

Therefore, to ensure that the young Kelleys of today know exactly what I think about *Black Marxism,* I now foreground my objection to the book—its duplicitous politics. Never ever do the names Malcolm X, Maurice Bishop, nor Thomas Sankara appear in its pages or in Robinson's Preface to the 2000 reissue.[13] Should I repeat that? Robinson, in omitting Bishop, as I elaborate in chapter 5, consciously rejected the apotheosis of the Black revolutionary experience as it unfolded in real time when writing his book. At least Robinson was consistent; he also rejected the proletariat's revolutionary potential, the core assumption of the authentic Marxist project.

Kelley, who would have been about nineteen at the time Maurice Bishop's and the New Jewel Party's Grenada Revolution commenced, might be forgiven for not having it on his youthful radar. The revolution's absence, however, along with the names of Malcolm and Sankara, in Kelley's forewords to the subsequent editions of *Black Marxism,* is inexcusable. In the era of Trump, which cries out for a working-class alternative, the last thing that toilers today need is something they *think* is revolutionary—a "wholly original theory of revolution," claims Kelley in 2021[14]—but is just the opposite. Believing so can be dangerous—as I explain in chapter 5.

About the same time that I got an advance copy of *Black Marxism* from *JAM* to review, the twenty-two-or-so-old Kelley also received a copy to do the same for the UCLA-based journal *Ufahamu.* Kelley never wrote his review. It was, he later admitted, a task for which he felt he was not then equipped.[15] For me, conversely, I relished the challenge. And it wasn't just because of birth-date privilege that I could do what Kelley could not, but because I had encountered, luckily, a decade earlier—as detailed in chapter 1 and what Kelley could only wish for[16]—the authentic Marxist project; hence, the confidence to take on Robinson. Two decades later, Kelley did write a review—his enthusiastic and influential foreword to the reissue of Robinson's book. Now that my 1985 review is back in print, readers can compare and determine which of the two reviews got Robinson right. The same can be done with West's effusive 1988 review of *Black Marxism*.

Deeply buried in almost one hundred pages of notes to *Black Marxism*—what I also missed in my 1985 review—Robinson revealed what he knew, or thought he did, about the Marxist project. Unlike Engels, he claimed, neither Marx, Lenin, nor Trotsky "seems to have given over much time to the study of working classes . . . This raises again the question: is Marxism a theory for the proletariat or of the proletariat?"[17] If not for the indispensable lessons not only about but *for* the proletariat, distilled by the three apparently negligent figures that Robinson singled out—a charge that's almost embarrassingly ill-informed—namely, the authentic Marxist project, this collection could not have been written.

Except for minor corrections and stylistic changes, also reformatting, the previously published essays in this collection are reproduced as they originally appeared but with updated endnotes. The help of Kyle Edwards, my Marx-Douglass book co-author, in doing so—along with substantive comments and suggestions—proved to be indispensable.

Lastly, to whet the reader's appetite for what follows, a bit of bonus, or "lagniappe," as some of us from New Orleans say. For those curious about the accuracy of AI, ChatGPT supplies an answer to the query "August Nimtz on Robinson's Black Marxism." The one it offers at the end of summer 2025 isn't bad, maybe a C+—certainly better than Google Scholar. The A-grade answer, however, awaits the patient reader of this collection.

We'll see how quickly the AI computers read—and maybe *understand*—once this book is in print.

1

Fortuitous Biography as Prelude

WE DON'T GET TO CHOOSE our biological parents, when we are born, or where. But such accidents of life can be determinant. Or, as Karl Marx once famously put it: "Men make their own history, but they do not make it as they please; they do not make it under self-selected circumstances, but under circumstances existing already, given and transmitted from the past."[1]

New Orleans, some of us natives say, half-jokingly—but with more than a grain of truth—is the northernmost city in the Caribbean. Along with its exceptional roots and culture comes another characteristic that distinguishes the Crescent City from virtually all the neighboring hinterlands of the old Confederacy. Unlike the latter, dominated by the racial dichotomy of the plantation, the heterogeneity of New Orleans, the largest city in the antebellum South, one intimately tied to global capitalism—ensured that the intersection of race and class would have more salience there than elsewhere in the region. Confederate rule, based on racial slavery, lasted no more than a year in the city, when Union capture in May 1862 quickly allowed the logic of class to reassert itself in a new and unencumbered way that has prevailed ever since.[2] Marx, who wrote about that moment, the Second American Revolution or the U.S. Civil War, has taught me that I'm very much a product of that liberatory project in my accidental place of birth and rearing.

Although my first participation in an antiracist protest occurred in 1954, when I was in the seventh grade (more about that shortly), only in 1956 did I become conscious of being a witness to something rebellious.[3] The Senate Internal Security Subcommittee, counterpart to the Cold War inquisition residing in the notorious House Un-American Activities Committee, held hearings in New Orleans to investigate "communist" influence in its labor movement, specifically, the influential, all-Black International Longshoremen's Association, Local 1419.[4] The union's presidents, Black household names, played a major role in the fight for Black representation and equality in the city—they were trade union leaders, in other words, unique in the Jim Crow South.[5]

E. Belfield Spriggins, trade unionist, NAACP activist, jazz cognoscente, and my high school art teacher, took me to see one of the hearings, a few blocks away from McDonogh No. 35, New Orleans' only downtown high school.[6] Mesmerizing was the Black witness who refused to be cowed about his alleged communist affiliations by the hostile questions of the committee's chairman, Mississippi's Democratic Party senator James Eastland. One of the state's major cotton barons, Eastland personified official white supremacy.

Forever etched on my brain is the image of this combative witness who argued vigorously with Eastland and bravely declined to take the Fifth Amendment.[7] If the racists loathed the communists, my juvenile enemy-of-my-enemy thinking concluded, then there must be something good about the Reds—and a Black one to boot. A 2019 *New York Times* obituary taught me for the first time the full name and the fascinating story of the witness, Jack Pitts O'Dell. The obit also came with almost unbelievable lagniappe, a photo of O'Dell's testimony—an image I had thought until then had only existed in my childhood memory. But no: the public record stored what I had witnessed some seven decades earlier. My first Black hero, it turned out, had indeed been a member of the Communist Party USA.[8]

Whether it was because of the hearing or not, I had a discussion with my mother around about that time about "socialism." As I plumb my memory banks, I suspect that it might have been the brutal murder of Emmett Till, four hours away in Mississippi, a week before my thirteenth birthday in 1955, that provoked the conversation. There was an air of despondency that hung over our household, as well as countless others. "Could there ever be equality for Negroes in America?" was the substance of the question I put to my mother. For which I had an answer. Only in a socialist society, it seemed to me, because it promised equality, could that be possible. I wanted to know what my mother thought. I honestly can't remember her reply, only that she didn't object to my argument. Thus, I had license—at least I thought so—to entertain the socialist alternative. Hence, by the time I heard O'Dell, I was probably predisposed to be sympathetic to his testimony.

Unbeknownst to me, Mr. Spriggins must have had my parents' permission—my mother's, most likely—to take a thirteen-year-old, in the depths of the Cold War, 1956, to such an event. He collaborated, I later learned, with her around trade union work—the Black teachers union in New Orleans and related civil rights campaigns. They, along with scores of other activists, especially those in the NAACP, had helped organize the protest I participated in two years earlier in 1954. Not coincidentally, my maternal grandmother, a domestic worker and NAACP activist, helped, also in 1956, to shield the membership lists of the organization from the prying eyes of racist state authorities—a testament, as I later came to appreciate, to the proletarian character of the civil rights movement, the Second Reconstruction,[9] an indispensable and tragically missing element in the First Reconstruction.

The catalyst for the 1954 protest was the annual commemoration, every May Day, public school children throughout the city were expected to pay homage to McDonogh with parades to his monument. But, if you were a Black child in Jim Crow New Orleans, that meant waiting, often in the hot sun, for the white students to go first to the monument before you could do the same. That year, Black parents, teachers, trade unionists, and civil rights activists said, No more. "This 'stunning display of solidarity,'" according to historian Kim Lacy Rogers, "was 'the first mass protest by New Orleans' Negro community.'"[10] That the action occurred two weeks before the historic Supreme Court *Brown v. Board of Education* decision was no coincidence—in anticipation of the Second Reconstruction.

Unforgettable, on May 17, 1954, was Mrs. Barnes, the teacher who came into our seventh-grade classroom at Valena C. Jones Elementary School to announce that the Supreme Court had just declared that racial segregation in public schools was unconstitutional—illegal, in other words. We all cheered! In that moment, there was no question or doubt, we felt, about the need to end the two-tiered system of public education in New Orleans that privileged some students at the expense of the others. The mass protest that we'd participated in two weeks earlier was exactly about that fact. We all thought, naively, the advantage of hindsight, that we'd be sitting next year in classrooms with students we'd been forcibly segregated from. Five years later, when I graduated from McDonogh No. 35, I was still in a segregated classroom. Thus, one of my first civics lessons: Never confuse a Supreme Court decision with its actual execution.

Yet an important breakthrough in the fight against Jim Crow did take place, the consequences of which I only now appreciate, due to its personal impact. An oddity about the racial regime in New Orleans is that while public schools were segregated, the public libraries—at least, after 1955, the year I first attended McDonogh No. 35—were not. Working largely out of public view, the NAACP's and other Black leaders successfully convinced the local ruling class that year to end Jim Crow in the public library system.[11] Because of that victory, a whole new world, literally, opened to me. Less than a fifteen-minute walk away from my school—the only Black high school so located—I now had access to the main public library, one of the largest book collections in the state. To be able to browse in the stacks was pure heaven. My intellectual horizons broadened like never before.

But that victory, I have also now learned, came with a price. The proviso in the Black-white elite deal to desegregate New Orleans public libraries stipulated that

> no publicity must follow. Instead . . . call the principals of the Negro high schools and tell them, "Did you know the library is open to Negroes now? If you have some students who want to go to the library, tell them to go to Latter [one of the previous all-white libraries]." Nothing was ever published in the newspapers.[12]

Clear now is why my closest high school friend, Nathaniel Hendricks, and I never encountered any other Blacks in the library. And with access to the stacks, as I now realize, we were less likely to spend time in the main reading room, where we would have been more visible to white patrons. We were, hence, two of the few lucky students who were told about the treasure trove that awaited us—a reality check about the dismantling of Jim Crow, at least in that stage of the process. The only irritant visiting the library—I'd forgotten about the separate restrooms and water fountains—was having to see the Robert E. Lee statue perched high on a column across the street—now stored in a city warehouse.

Also unbeknownst at the time to me about Mr. Spriggins, is that he recruited me to the Second Reconstruction, the civil rights movement. At the end of the school day, in that same first year of high school, I accompanied him many a day to the voter registration office, also a few blocks away, to count the number of Blacks registered in New Orleans. Evidently—what I surmised years later since nothing was really explained to me, at least as far as I can remember—the NAACP had won the right to look at the registration books to try to prove systemic racial discrimination.[13] Characteristic of a real social movement, something I learned decades later, is that it sweeps into its ranks many who aren't even aware they are a participant—exactly my experience in regard to the Second Reconstruction.

Like my mother, my father was a trade union activist, perhaps for familial reasons. In 1918, his father, a fireman on the Southern Railway, joined with other Black workers, including an older son, to act collectively to address work-related inequities under the Jim Crow regime—a role model, in other words, for his son.[14] Both of my parents served at one time or another as presidents of their all-Black locals. During the Second World War, in Hawthorn, Nevada, where the family was living, the two of them helped found an NAACP branch—a response to the police victimization of young Black women.[15] In anticipation of their later joint activism.

Toward the end of his life, my father explained, in an interview I conducted, why he stepped down as the president of his local of the Black employees union at the historic U.S. Custom House.[16] When the opportunity arose, sometime during the Second Reconstruction, to merge the all-white and all-Black locals into one local, his Black co-unionists objected, against his recommendation to do so. Rebuffed, my father decided to step down. Though I had not known that fact, I had evidently been imbued with the instinct of unifying the working class, regardless of other identities.[17] Whatever the case, trade union consciousness, inherently a class question, informed my political formation from both sides of the household.

Organized resistance evidently came early in my father's life. Also, toward the end of his life, I learned that he'd been expelled from college during his first year, Xavier University, a Black Catholic institution in New Orleans, for helping to organize a protest. The racist white nuns, in his opinion, who administered the school deserved to be challenged. My radical proclivities came, as my mother used to say, "honestly."

New Orleans also uniquely taught what would later become *de rigueur* in the academy: If skin color was real, race was an invention. To grow up in the upper Seventh Ward, known for its Black Creole residents, and hear about the *passé blancs*, rumored or real, living nearby—so different from the uptown neighborhood of Gert Town where I first lived—made it easy for me to later understand the constructed character of race. To have had classmates and childhood friends who were phenotypically Caucasian but, under Louisiana's racist "one-drop rule," classified as Black like me, made that possible.[18] That part of the city taught that the Black-white racial dichotomy, hegemonic elsewhere, was inadequate in making sense of social reality. Not unlike most of the Caribbean and Latin America, it was more complicated. The exception within the exception. And, with a paternal grandfather whose parents were of German—hence my last name—and

Choctaw origin but who identified as "Black," I intuited the inventiveness of "race" at a very early age.

Arguably the most consequential reading of my high school years—what hindsight teaches—helping to make sense of another dimension of New Orleans' social complexity, was E. Franklin Frazier's 1957 classic *Black Bourgeoisie*.[19] Though my working-class family didn't belong to the New Orleans edition of that milieu, we were certainly connected with it through educational networks and thus conscious of its influence. Frazier's critical depiction and explanation of the milieu's modus operandi resonated with me. In New Orleans, interestingly, owing to its large working-class Black Creole population, fair skin color, unlike in many other U.S. cities, was not a necessary predictor for membership in that privileged social layer. To have since learned that Frazier's book significantly influenced Malcolm X—inspiration it seems for his oft-made "house Negro" versus "field Negro" distinction—was a truly joyous discovery.[20]

Decisive also in my political trajectory is what transpired four hundred miles from New Orleans on January 1, 1959. Cuba had long been on my radar ever since I could appreciate the significance of the map. To my north was the epitome of racial dichotomy, Mississippi and northern Louisiana, where white supremacy, I imagined, ruled with abandon, as in the case of Emmett Till's murder. But if I looked southward, across the Caribbean, I could see, and not just imagine, a much more tolerant world for people who resembled me. No wonder that Havana, especially Centro Habana, with its rainbow skin colors, seemed so familiar to me when I visited briefly in 1990 and later was a resident there for six months between 2006 and 2007. Never have I felt so inconspicuous and thus at home when abroad.

Fueling that sense of being part of a much larger world was New Orleans' historical and continuous connection to Cuba from which the Spanish once administered the city (its founding charter is still in Havana). Family friends and neighbors who worked as merchant marines could show us things and regale our young ears with stories about that other world, no doubt in hindsight, cultivating an early curiosity about what lay beyond the shores of the United States. And to realize that people who looked like me were not a minority of the world but maybe a *majority*, was truly liberating.

My youthful love affair with everything Cuban, sports, music—including a sixth-grade crush on a red-haired *mulata* émigrée—therefore predisposed me to embrace the process that Fidel Castro inaugurated. Revolution, the overturning of things—what we needed in Jim Crow New Orleans—was exactly, I imagined, what seemed to be going on four hundred miles away in the Caribbean. The embrace has never ceased.

Also on my radar, owing largely to my mother, was the African independence movement. When Ghana became independent in 1957, she organized my sister and me to do a presentation to our high school classes, accompanied by a show-and-tell of things long forgotten. Thus, I was primed to be open to the next major chapter in that development, the South African Sharpeville Massacre in March 1960, when police killed dozens of Africans peacefully protesting the apartheid regime's hated passbook laws.

Especially striking about the South African reality for me was its resemblance to our own struggle. *Drum* magazine, Johannesburg-based and reminiscent of *Ebony* (and accidentally discovered in the library at Purdue University where I was now enrolled), taught that fact. Though familiar with the key struggles of the Second Reconstruction, the 1955 Montgomery bus boycott and the 1957 school desegregation battle in Little Rock, and an occasional participant, I found more attractive developments abroad—evidence that our struggle here was part of something larger.

One of those occasional moments continues to have currency. For about a week in late summer 1964 in New Orleans, I attended a workshop to learn how to register to vote, to successfully answer, particularly, a long application form designed to make sure that people who had my skin color would not be able to register. I learned later that the civil rights movement leadership, nationally and locally, had decided that year to suspend the public protests it had been organizing—one at which I participated in 1962—and focus on voting registration. Making sure that Barry Goldwater, the Republican Party presidential candidate—and no friend of Black people—would be defeated by Lyndon Johnson, the Democratic Party incumbent, was the priority. For me, Johnson was the lesser evil I had long been suspicious of, thinking erroneously that he'd been a Klan member. I'd hold my nose and vote for him.

After arriving at the registration office—where I had once counted with Mr. Spriggins the number of Blacks registered in New Orleans—and then handing an official my just-filled-out registration form, I waited, confident that I'd successfully navigated the obstacle course, while he looked at it. Pointing to some questions, he asked, "Why didn't you answer these ones?" "Because," I said, "they didn't apply to me." "Then, you should have drawn a line in the space," he gruffly replied. "Come back in two weeks and try again."

That was impossible, because classes were about to begin at Howard University, where I was now enrolled in graduate school in African Studies. The first time, then, that I tried to vote, albeit for a bourgeois candidate, I was denied the opportunity. Thus, it was the racist system that made it possible for me to say—with some pride—that I have never done so.

The Sharpeville Massacre grabbed my attention, prompting me to give my first written speech, in Speech 101, at Purdue

University. Four years later, spring 1964, I participated in the first political action for which I had organizational responsibilities—a picket line in front of the White House to protest the trial of Nelson Mandela and co-defendants charged with sabotage against the South African regime. The multiracial action, also a first for me, included students from southern Africa studying at D.C.-area colleges. Leslie Rubin, one of .my professors at Howard and a white South African, recruited me to the anti-apartheid movement, my first organized political work.

The interracial character of the picket line is noteworthy, because three years later I was no longer disposed to engage in a similar kind of action. A year after the very multiracial anti-apartheid conference I attended in Washington, March 1965, which proved to be the initiation of the South African divestment movement in the United States,[21] another political decision was made hundreds of miles away, which, as I've only recently come to appreciate, significantly impacted me and my Black age cohorts—white ones as well.

The Student Nonviolent Coordinating Committee's expulsion in 1966 of its white members not only convulsed the organization itself—and its individuals—but had ramifications far beyond its ranks. The decision complemented its new "Black Power" perspective that new leader Stokely Carmichael/Kwame Toure championed.[22] Owing to the moral authority that SNCC—heroes and heroines for all of us of a similar age—had earned in the trenches of the Second Reconstruction, the decision became emulative. At Indiana University in Bloomington (I.U.) where I was now studying for a doctorate in African politics, I voted with the majority in our Black graduate student organization that involvement in personal relationships with Caucasians was incompatible with membership, resulting in the exclusion of at least one member.

Until SNCC's 1966 decision, antiracist work in the United States had mostly been interracial, going back at least to the antebellum abolitionists, if not earlier, a fact that most, if not all, African Americans agreed with. It was part of the reason why many of us in that era had greeted approvingly Malcolm X's rethinking of his race-exclusionary stance after his second visit to Mecca in 1964. We all paid close attention to this, but with Malcolm's assassination in February 1965, his revisionist trajectory was tragically cut short. The race sectarian posture, epitomized by Elijah Muhammad's Nation of Islam, thus had free rein to become hegemonic. It informed, if not directly, progressive work elsewhere, as in the case of our Black graduate student organization at I.U. The SNCC decision continues to reverberate. The oft-done practice in Black Lives Matter circles to relegate white supporters to second-class status constitutes an echo, I argue, of SNCC's fateful decision. And one that runs counter to the course Malcolm was on at the end of his life.[23]

Fortunately, my embrace of sectarian Black nationalism didn't last very long. I was soon cured of its allure by my stay in Tanzania, where I went in 1969, as a Black nationalist/Pan-Africanist, to do dissertation research on Islam and politics. Seventeen months later, I left in search of the communist alternative. If Tanzania, the headquarters of the Southern African liberation movement, was the best that the African Revolution had to offer in 1969–1970, then clearly something more radical was required.

Briefly, the emerging class inequalities and their consequences that were increasingly on display after Tanzania's independence in 1961 could not be easily explained away by the all-so-real race and ethnic realities still in place. A new ruling class in Black skin now had agency to call the shots, and it performed as ruling classes had always done. Frantz Fanon's Marxist-informed book, *The Wretched of the Earth*, had bequeathed to us a decade earlier the label for this new class, "a national bourgeoisie." It seemed apt for what I witnessed in Tanzania.

Tanzania's capital, Dar es Salaam, including its university, provided me with resources not only for writing a dissertation but also for political clarity.[24] The opportunity and privilege of meeting and hearing revolutionaries and revolutionary scholars like Mohamed Babu, Marcelino dos Santos, Walter Rodney, and John Saul convinced me that the best I could do for the African Revolution was to return to the United States and make a revolution there—however unsure I was what that meant. That conclusion, combined with all of my earlier autobiography, explains why—admittedly, again in hindsight—I was ripe for the picking in 1971.

Both Cedric Robinson and I—born two years apart in the early 1940s, both B.A. graduates in 1963—spent time in Africa: he as an undergraduate at Berkeley; I as a graduate student at I.U. With similar political backgrounds, I suspect that when, where, and how long we lived in Africa proved determinant in our different political paths. Robinson was a 1962 summer-long community development volunteer in pre-independence Zimbabwe.[25] Seven years later, I was a seventeen-month dissertation researcher in Tanzania. In other words, I had the good luck to witness what the African independence struggle, arguably the continent's best, had, after almost a decade, delivered—an authentic national bourgeoisie and, most significantly, a credible critique of that outcome. Robinson, conversely, had the luxury of imagining something more revolutionary, as he completed *Black Marxism* only two years into Zimbabwe's independence—before the country's descent into something qualitatively worse than postcolonial Tanzania.

Solely for intellectual reasons did I decide to take a teaching job in political science at the University of Minnesota.[26] Logical positivism best describes my then theoretical orientation, and the university was a well-known center for pursuing that perspective. Completely unfamiliar to me, however, when I moved there in September 1971, and where I knew no one, was Minnesota's rich history of class struggle.

As the first Black member in the department, I would be an "affirmative action" hire, the department chair told me during my job interview. I had no idea whether he meant that as a compliment or not, but I took it that way.[27] My hiring registered, I assumed, a victory in the struggle my generation had recently waged to get predominantly white campuses to employ people who looked like me. For that reason, I felt that I had a moral obligation, once on board at Minnesota, to make sure that I continued to be an activist in the Black community, both on and off campus. If "the movement" had made it possible for me to get the job, then at least being available to the movement was obligatory. Subsequent generations of Black hires, having no direct ties to those earlier struggles, are less likely to have that same sense of obligation. Individual rather than collective achievements have, in general, more value for them.

Having just collaborated with other Black graduate students at Indiana University on Angela Davis defense work, I tried, shortly after my arrival in Minneapolis, to find the Communist Party USA, but without success. Later, I learned why: they were deeply buried in Minnesota's Democratic Farmer-Labor Party, still carrying out their decades-long popular front policy. If the CP was hard to find, another party, which I'd never heard of, was visible within days of my arrival. A young person, maybe seventeen years old, easily convinced me to buy an introductory subscription to *The Militant*. The paper was familiar because I had found it useful for putting together a fact sheet about the Davis case—one of my defense committee tasks—it was even better, I thought, than the

CP's *Daily World*. But I didn't know who published it; it could have been, given the expanding women's movement, "a women's lib" rag?—a patronizing label that the youth, women especially, quickly taught me to forgo. It turned out the Socialist Workers Party published *The Militant*.

Until meeting the Socialist Workers Party (SWP), the only white radicals I'd known were on the campus at I.U. Before graduating from Purdue in 1963, I signed up for the Northern Student Movement, the interracial northern ally of SNCC, but was never integrated into the organization during my stay in the Chicago area that summer.[28] Working in a steel mill in East Chicago, Indiana, to save money to go to graduate school, I had, for the first time, white co-workers. The summertime experience allowed me to get a glimpse of working-class solidarity across racial lines when an older white worker, noting, on my first day on the job, that I was trying too hard to impress a supervisor with my "broomology skills"—as Malcolm would have aptly put it[29]—approached me and said, "Look, son, we don't work that hard around here; slow down." That got a big laugh out of my parents when I told them at the end of the summer.

It took a Militant Labor Forum, the SWP weekly public event in fall 1971 for me to hear for the first time a revolutionary worker "in white skin"—as Marx might have put it—a railroad worker, what my grandfather had been. Most impressive was the topic of the forum, the then unfolding Pakistani Bangladeshi war. The speaker, Charlie Scheer, without professorial credentials or pretensions, helped me to make sense of the ongoing tragedy. His talk was mind expanding—offering an explanation I couldn't find at the university where I was now teaching. An "American white worker" not only interested in what was taking place on the other side of the planet, in the "Third World," but able to make sense of it.

To also learn that several individuals, also Caucasian, in subsequent audiences in that same Minneapolis venue had been communist revolutionaries since the 1930s was especially rewarding. Two of them, Jake Cooper and Harry DeBoer, had been bodyguards for Leon Trotsky in Mexico, and later served time in a U.S. prison for their beliefs.[30] So impressed, I invited the two to address one of my classes. For the first time, I was encountering not campus radicals but rather the real "radical" thing. "Whither the white proletariat?" "Did it have revolutionary potential?" These questions, at the heart of the race-versus-class debate in the United States, were being answered for me in the flesh.

The Trotskyist current that the SWP then represented in the world communist movement had more prominence in Minneapolis than anywhere else, thus making it easier for me—by good fortune—to find an answer to the race-class debate. My quest for the communist alternative to politics as usual was now being fulfilled, enough to convince me inside of a year to join the Party in 1972, where I remained until 1995.[31] Given my Angela Davis defense work, had I not accidentally found one of Trotsky's currents, I would have in all likelihood ended up in the CPUSA or one of the many incarnations of Stalinism—and years later probably in denial or embarrassed for having done so.

Joining the SWP, becoming the only Black member of maybe a seventy-five-person branch, was a relatively easy decision, since I knew no one in Minnesota before arriving. I had no social ties there, both in terms of class and race, that would have precluded being in a predominantly white communist organization. Thus, I could reinvent myself. Besides, if I was willing to be the only Black member of the University of Minnesota's political science department, why not do the same in a revolutionary party? Being an "affirmative action hire," as I interpreted it, gave license to that decision.

In 1979, my mother, the original "helicopter mom" I'm convinced, paid an unexpected visit to the SWP national headquarters in New York City, where I was on staff at *The Militant*.[32] After taking her on a tour of the five-story building in the Lower West Side of Manhattan (I instinctively knew that's what she wanted), beginning with the library at the top, she—a Black working-class fighter born in 1912 and reared in Jim Crow Louisiana; a teacher; a principal; a University of Chicago M.A. graduate—looked at her forty-year-old son and said: "Now look, boy, you pay attention to these white folks; they know what they're doing." Once embarrassed, I proudly recount that moment.

Relevant for this collection of writings is the educational campaign the SWP launched in 1978, to have its members collectively read and study Marx, Engels, and Lenin in their own words. Most of us had known those three figures largely through Trotsky's lens. The intent of the project was to politically prepare members for the concomitant campaign to get most of them into industrial jobs, "the turn." The first article in this collection, my 1985 critique of *Black Marxism*, was the first product of that campaign. When writing it, I didn't seek feedback from any comrades, so I can't claim that it represented Party thinking at the time, but I think, or would like to believe, that it would have passed muster with the leadership.

No longer in the SWP after 1995, I had the time and privilege to do a deep dive into the collected works of Marx and Engels, and Lenin, initially employing the syllabi the Party had put together (biweekly Cuba solidarity work constitutes since then my organized political regimen). The first book, in 2000, *Marx and Engels: Their Contribution to the Democratic Breakthrough*, continues to be the only detailed treatment of Marx and Engels as political activists. All of my writings, including the essays in this collection, seek to distill the political lessons that Marx and Engels bequeathed in their five-decades-long activism.

Had it not been, then, for the opportunity and good luck to function for almost a quarter-century in a collective, mostly disciplined fashion in a Leninist party, in the laboratory of the class struggle— to test the lessons of that rich communist bequest—the 2000 book and subsequent ones, and articles, including those in this collection, could not have been written. This is an experience to which I'm forever indebted.

All these writings intend to empower the working class *as a class* when it says it's had enough—when no one can predict. Resolving the time-worn race-class debate will figure decisively in that moment. For the U.S. reality, it can't be otherwise and thus has world-history repercussions. This collection constitutes an intervention in that debate, part of the necessary preparatory work for our species doing something it's never done before—putting an end, not only to racial inequality but, most consequentially, to class society, the operating system upon which social inequalities rest.

Lest it be assumed that the early years of this narrative are about an inevitable march to the communist alternative, let this coda—especially for youthful eyes—suggest otherwise.

As a B.A. graduate, an international relations major, from Purdue in 1963, I dutifully tried to do what IR majors did in those days, enter the U.S. Foreign Service. But I was unable to achieve the required score above 69 on the admissions test. My earlier Jim Crow education, it seemed, had caught up with me. Reading the *New York Times* daily, front to back, I heard, would ensure passing the test. So, in early 1964, I read a *Times* article that the Ford Foundation was funding a program to recruit African Americans to enter the diplomatic corps—a vanguard meritocratic affirmative action project.[33] Evidently, the more farsighted of the U.S. ruling class, in the midst of the Cold War and the African Revolution, recognized that they had a problem: not enough apparatchiks in Black skin to advance Washington and Wall Street's agenda abroad.

Because Howard University would be the site for the initiative, I could make an in-person inquiry about the application process. I signed up for the required selection interview on a Saturday morning in late April or early May. But, for four consecutive nights prior to the interview, I treated myself, with a just-received income tax refund, to the Bohemian Caverns, a famed jazz nightclub on U Street in D.C. There, the one and only Thelonious Monk was performing maybe thirty feet away from the bar—where I sipped my then favorite spirit, Wild Turkey.[34] Come Saturday morning, I was in no shape to convince anyone that I'd be an effective emissary for Washington. Not surprisingly, I bombed the interview. Spectacularly.

Saved from the imperial project, it may be Thelonious Monk to whom I'm most indebted. Once again, good luck prevailed.

2

Black Marxism: The First In-Depth Review

Review: "Marxism and the Black Struggle: The 'Class v. Race' Debate Revisited" (1984). Originally published in the *Journal of African Marxists*.

WHEN EMMANUEL HANSEN, ONE THE editors of the *Journal of African Marxists,* a unique continental-wide vanguard initiative, asked me in 1984 to review Cedric Robinson's recently published *Black Marxism*—with which I was unfamiliar—I felt both honored and obligated. Hansen, originally from Ghana, and I had been classmates in graduate school in political science and African Studies at Indiana University in the late 1960s. Though only in occasional contact after then, he probably learned about my political trajectory afterwards from *JAM* collaborator Adele Jinadu, whose dissertation committee I served on in 1973 at the University of Minnesota.

By then, I was a public Marxist as a member of the Socialist Workers Party (SWP). Because membership often entailed, when possible, participation in Black nationalist organizations for its Black members, I quickly became familiar with the often intense, at times violent, class-versus-race debate that racked the milieu. Unlike the Communist Party (CPUSA), the other "old left" party, the SWP, gave critical support to Black nationalism, the legacy of its embrace of Malcolm X, even before his break with the Nation of Islam. For me as a new SWP member in Minnesota, there was the African Liberation Support Committee (ALSC), founded in 1972. At the historic ALSC conference in Frogmore, South Carolina, in the summer of 1973, seated next to me was Amiri Baraka, the leading cultural nationalist. I had a front row seat to that debate. The real question at stake, as it had once been for me, was always "Whither the American white proletariat?" Luckily, by the time I met the debate, I had already received an answer—in the flesh.

Though I didn't attend the event, I supported a Minnesota contingent of the U.S. delegation to the Sixth Pan African Congress in Dar es Salaam, Tanzania, in 1974, probably the high water mark of that phase of U.S. Black nationalism. Unreconstructed U.S. Black nationalists, those who prioritized skin color, met their defeat there. Revolutionaries in Africa, who had to deal with the real world of politics, rejected the criteria of skin color for making political judgments that were all so determinant for U.S. Black cultural nationalists.[1] The founding of *JAM* eight years later registered in many ways that victory. I was someone in the United States whom the editors knew would confront unreconstructed skin color nationalists. The defeat in Dar es Salaam explains why the cultural nationalists were largely absent from subsequent southern African solidarity work, to which I turned my attention—a movement too multiracial, in their worldview.[2]

In 1980, another nationalist formation emerged, the National Black Independent Political Party (NBIPP). Standing on the shoulders of the historic 1972 National Black Convention in Gary, Indiana, NBIPP pledged to realize Malcolm X's directive of independent Black political action, warranting, therefore,

Black SWP members to be part of that effort. For almost three years I served as the effective organizer of the Minnesota chapter, the second time I functioned as an open Marxist, but with more responsibilities, in Black nationalist circles. NBIPP, mostly moribund by 1984, was, in hindsight, the last real gasp of revolutionary Black nationalism.

When I came to Robinson's book, therefore, I had had a decade-long experience of defending, often alone, the Marxist perspective in the leading Black nationalist formations of that era, which included both cultural and revolutionary nationalists. That's what informed my opening comment in the review: "Because of the intensity of the debate in the last decade, Robinson, like many proponents of national analysis, has had to familiarize himself—if not always understand—class analysis. Thus, *Black Marxism* may be the most informed and sophisticated defense of the nationalist position."

Written in Pittsburgh sometime in 1984, the review reflects my then current political work. On leave from the University of Minnesota, I tried, unsuccessfully, as part of the SWP's turn to industry, to get employed in the coal industry. Just prior to moving there, I'd been active not only in NBIPP but also Grenada solidarity work, a multiracial effort. At the beginning of the year, I spent two weeks in Nicaragua on a solidarity work brigade doing what I jokingly called "my roots thing"—picking cotton on a recently Sandinista-nationalized cotton plantation. Proletarian internationalism, hence, weighed heavily on my mind when I wrote the review, which reflected what the real world of politics taught.

Not the least important fact about that moment for me was to witness the end of the "American Dream" for tens of thousands of "workers in white skin"—the deindustrialization of the American heartland, which was the then reality of Pittsburgh. That year-long experience, doing door to door sales of *The Militant*, the SWP newspaper, in white working-class neighborhoods, and attending meetings of the unemployed, offered in-flesh answers to the ever current "Whither the white proletariat" question. Learning that someone who looked like me could be welcomed in such spaces was a precious and unforgettable lesson.[3]

Beginning in 1979, the same year the Grenada and Sandinista revolutions triumphed—the biggest breakthrough in the world revolutionary movement since the Cuban triumph two decades earlier—the SWP launched an educational campaign for its members to read Marx, Engels, and Lenin in their own words. That project enabled me to see what was missing in Robinson's narrative, however erudite it at times read. Strikingly absent, I soon discovered, was any recognition of real-world politics, precisely because they did not lend themselves to his classless cultural nationalist worldview. Rather than deal with reality, Robinson and kindred spirits took refuge in the metaphysical stratosphere.

In case the reader detects impatience with Robinson by the end of the review, they're right. If the Grenada Revolution, arguably the apotheosis—even until today—of the diasporic Black revolutionary experience, a revolution alive and well when Robinson wrote his book, failed to make it into *Black Marxism*, then why the subtitle of the book, *The Making of the Black Radical Tradition*? Those of us who lived in that moment, who know the details and are still fortunately alive, were and are obligated to state the truth. Otherwise, we become unwitting enablers of thin gruel masquerading as revolutionary substance, ill-equipping the revolutionary-minded, especially the youth, to know "what is to be done" when the real moment occurs.[4] The omission of Grenada's history-making events in Robinson's narrative was—and remains—unpardonable, as well as instructive.[5]

Precisely because of the centrality of the "whither the American white proletariat" question in the Black nationalist debates then—and until today in one form or another—I purposely ended the review with the advice of Maurice Bishop, the leader of the Grenada Revolution.

> [I] . . . would very strongly recommend to the Black movement in America the importance of developing the firmest and closest links with the white working-class movement and the white progressive movement. Our feeling certainly is that in order to win that struggle inside of America, it's extremely important that all progressive forces get together and wage a consistent fight against the real enemy.

No wonder there is no mention of Grenada, an indisputably key moment in Black revolutionary politics, in Robinson's narrative about the "Black radical tradition." Inconvenient advice and facts for a cultural nationalist, as well as the fact that it was a Marxist venue, the SWP's Pathfinder Press, that published and still publishes Bishop's speeches.

Because Robinson and I were generational cohorts—he was born in1940, two years before me, the reader might wonder if the two of us ever met. We were members of a small, privileged group of African Americans, academics at prestigious white academies. No is the answer. But, if memory serves me four decades later, it's likely that we once saw one another, from a distance, at a meeting of the American Political Science Association in the late 1980s or early 1990s, thus, after the publication of my review of *Black Marxism*. And if I am remembering correctly, we pretended that we didn't see one another. Hence, I'll never know if he ever read and might have thought of my critical review of his book.

The *Journal of African Marxists* ceased publication about 1986. In his last letter to me, dated April 18, 1985, editor Hansen wrote in response to my inquiry: "Yes, I would be delighted to take a look at your Grenada paper. I am sure there is a lot for all of us to learn from that experience . . . We are . . . launching a new journal, *African Journal of Political Economy* . . . since *JAM*'s outlet is rather limited."[6] If cultural nationalists like Robinson had no interest in learning about the Grenada experience, genuine revolutionaries, like Hansen, had just the opposite attitude. They were hungry for lessons.[7] His second point in the letter likely explains, also, the lack of attention my review might have otherwise gotten. Shortly after *JAM*'s last issue, Hansen, born in 1937, died.[8] My review follows.

Review: "Marxism and the Black Struggle: The 'Class v. Race' Debate Revisited"

August H. Nimtz, Jr.

More than ten years ago Robert Allen wrote in his very popular *Black Awakening in Capitalist America* that the "long-standing unsolved problem" for Afro-American radicals "lies in finding the proper relationship between a purely national (or racial) analysis and program on the one hand, and a purely class analysis and program on the other."[9] Much has occurred in the Black American struggle since the appearance of Allen's book. But in one form or another the debate continues between proponents of both positions.

Cedric J. Robinson's *Black Marxism: The Making of the Black Radical Tradition* (London: Zed Books, 1983), the subject of this review article, can best be understood as part of this historical discussion. Contrary to what his title might suggest, Robinson sides with, if not a "purely national" analysis, then something fairly close. Because of the intensity of the debate in the last decade, Robinson, like many proponents of national analysis, has had to familiarize himself—if not always understand—class analysis. Thus, *Black Marxism* may be the most informed and sophisticated defense of the nationalist position. In spite of this, however, I argue that Robinson's thesis is flawed; his errors are common to the nationalist view when counterposed to a Marxist perspective.

Robinson argues that Marxism or historical materialism is a uniquely European ideology and as such is limited in its applicability to the world beyond Europe. Furthermore, its limitation is in time as well as space—nineteenth-century Europe. Given its origins, Marxism is, thus, burdened with the intellectual and cultural baggage of Europe. The most important of these from Robinson's perspective is racism.[10] As petit bourgeois intellectuals, Marx and Engels failed to explain the persistence of racism and in the process erroneously attributed a progressive role to capitalism and the bourgeoisie in its eradication. They also overestimated the ability of Europe's proletariat to overcome this legacy. By not understanding the extent to which they themselves were products of that heritage, Marx and Engels were unable to fully appreciate the nationalism of the oppressed in the non-Western world, and in particular, the Black radical tradition.

Because of its African origins, the latter has a radically different outlook from that of historical materialism. The result is that the articulation of the Black radical tradition has had to involve a conscious break with the Marxist perspective. As evidence, Robinson draws on the intellectual and political development of three leading Black radicals—W. E. B. Du Bois, C. L. R. James, and Richard Wright—whose "apprenticeships" as Marxists "proved to be significant but ultimately unsatisfactory."[11]

Before critically examining this argument, a general observation about its overall validity is in order. It is not clear if Robinson intends to "prove" his thesis with these three cases or if he is merely illustrating it. If the former is his intent, immediate questions must be raised about the representativeness of his examples. There are other Black radicals who had Marxist "apprenticeships"—Fanon, for example—who might also have been looked at. Even if his objective is illustrative, he is still on shaky terrain since it is debatable that two of the three, Du Bois and James, ever broke with Marxism. Du Bois died a member of the American Communist Party and James, as far as this reviewer knows, still considers himself a Marxist.[12] Although these objections might constitute a fatal blow against Robinson's argument, it would be a mistake to dismiss beforehand what he has to say. His history, for example, of Black radical activities in the diaspora in Part Two is an important contribution to the literature.

This review cannot address all the issues that Robinson raises in his 452-page work. The primary focus is on his critique of what Marx and Engels wrote in relation to his overall thesis.

Part One of the book, "The Emergence and Limitations of European Radicalism," presents Robinson's critique. His analysis of the historical materialist method, the nature of capitalism, and the proletariat and the national question are the most important issues here because they all surface in one way or another throughout the volume.

In his claim that historical materialism is limited to nineteenth century Europe, Robinson cites Engels for support. In his famous letter to Joseph Bloch in 1890 in which he outlines the basic ideas of historical materialism, Engels points out that all human activity, including ideas, are historically specific, subject not only to economic conditions—"ultimately decisive"—but "the political ones . . . and indeed even the traditions which haunt human minds . . ." as well.[13] Robinson correctly notes that this observation could apply equally to the ideas of Marx and Engels. "[T]heir work, itself the critique of bourgeois society and industrial capitalism, would someday—when the material forces of society had progressed beyond their stage of development in the 19th Century—be subject to criticism(negation)."[14] What Robinson is saying here—a major assumption of his argument—is that nineteenth-century European capitalism has undergone changes of such a degree that its fundamental features are qualitatively different from what Marx and Engels analyzed.

While Robinson cites Engels in his defense, his methodology is quite the opposite of the latter. In a most revealing statement early in his book, he writes, "The history of capitalism has in no way distinguished itself from earlier eras with respect to wars, material crises and social conflicts."[15] He presents virtually no data to support this very sweeping assertion. Throughout the work his tendency is to assign low priority if any to the material world. His method is that of an idealist. Thus, ideas are seldom tested in terms of the material reality to which they refer.

There is no disputing that capitalism has significantly changed since the publication of *Capital*. To say, however, that the capitalism of today is no longer amenable to its analysis is a question of fact that has to be proved. It is not hyperbole to say that the most salient feature of the world today is the international capitalist crisis. Such crises, Marx discovered, are fundamentally crises of overproduction. Can Robinson deny that the 1974–75 crisis and the current one that most of the capitalist world remains in are basically what Marx described and explained?[16]

Capitalist crises are not only still with us, but they are increasingly more profound as Marx said would be the case. He also predicted that they would have a more international character; no area of the world—the Black world included—would be immune to the penetration of capitalist relations of production as well as any arena within society. Again, can Robinson deny this reality?

In arguing that historical materialism has limited relevance in the semicolonial and colonial world, Robinson correctly points out that Marx and Engels intended that their analysis of the rise of capitalism apply only to Western Europe. He errs in interpreting this caveat to mean that their methodology has no applicability to the so-called third world. Marx thought that his most important discoveries were: "1) that the *existence of classes* is merely linked to the *particular historical phases in the development of production,* 2) that class struggle necessarily leads to the *dictatorship of the proletariat,* 3) that this dictatorship itself only constitutes the transition to the *abolition of all classes* and to a *classless society*" (italics in original).[17]

Robinson must certainly recognize that there are third world revolutionaries and intellectuals who have consciously and successfully employed this framework in analyzing their own societies. This was the perspective that informed Walter Rodney, clearly in his *How Europe Underdeveloped Africa.*[18] A more recent example of a work that also focuses on Africa is A. M. Babu's *African Socialism or Socialist Africa?*[19] about which more will be said later.

Even if a case could be made that historical materialism has limited relevance in analyzing third world societies at some earlier stage in their development, it flies in the face of reality to suggest as Robinson does that such is the case today. Whatever their different historical paths of development, these regions are today as profoundly subjected to the exigencies of capitalism as the European centers from which it originated—from the reproduction of the class structure of capitalist Europe to the devastating effects of its crises; in the case of the latter, even more so.

Part of Robinson's problem is conceptual in inadequately defining capitalism and distinguishing it from preexisting economic systems. Related to this is his claim that capitalism originated much earlier than what Marx proposed. This allows him to substantiate a key plank in his argument, that is, Marx overestimated the progressive character of capitalism.

Obviously, capitalist relations of production existed as early as the fifteenth century as Robinson claims. As a mode of production, however, capitalism only arises when generalized commodity production appears. In conjunction with this process is the appearance of the proletariat that not only has to sell its labor for its survival—unlike other subject classes—but provides a market for commodities. What made generalized commodity production possible for the first time in human history was industrialization, which reduced drastically the costs of production and, thus, created a mass market. This was quite different from mercantile capitalism, which Robinson seems to equate with the capitalist mode of production. As Marx discovered, the inherent quality of a commodity—the embodiment of both use and exchange values—is a fundamental cause of capitalist crises. Whereas previous economic crises stemmed from societies not having enough, those associated with capitalism result from too many commodities having been produced at the prices capitalists demand.

For this mode of production to have become a reality, it was necessary that the coercive power of the state be employed. Thus, while capitalist activities certainly existed as early as Robinson argues, it is only when capital captures state power—imposes the dictatorship of the bourgeoisie—that its successful development is assured. It is for these reasons—industrialization and the bourgeois revolutions—that Marx dated capitalism's appearance as a mode of production in the second half of the eighteenth century.

To support his claim that Marx and Engels overestimated capitalism's progressive side, which was reflected in their insensitivity to Europe's racist legacy, Robinson dismisses its material achievements. In so doing, he strips historical materialism of an essential tenet, for that is precisely what they recognized as capitalism's raison d'etre. Its productive forces surpassed all previous and existing modes of production. Can Robinson really deny this fact? Most importantly, capitalism provided for the first time in human history the possibility of eliminating want and, thus, inequality. In other words, it created the material basis for socialist society.

Marx and Engels argued that capitalism was by and large incompatible with preexisting modes of production and would either undermine them or transform them for its own needs. A major contention of Robinson, however, particularly in Part Two of his book, is that it did not "result [in] the elimination or curtailment of slavery," an example of its nonprogressive character.[20] He rests his case largely on the fact that capitalism, which he says appeared in the fifteenth century, was directly linked to modern slavery in the West. He acknowledges that Marx stressed the importance of slavery for capitalism's development. Marx, he says, only emphasized slavery's role in primitive accumulation while a more correct analysis would show that it was a necessary component of capitalism fully developed.

It is a fact that industrial capital played a leading role in the fight against slavery that began at the end of the eighteenth century. Robinson recognizes this but evidently does not see any contradiction with his above-quoted assessment.[21] From his perspective, apparently, since mercantile capitalism, which he equates with the capitalist mode of production, was linked so long to slavery, it was inconsequential what industrial capital later did.

Although Robinson fails to explain why industrial capital opposed slavery—more correctly, chattel slavery—Marx was very clear on this. Mechanization, which brought about generalized commodity production, has as its goal the ceaseless economizing of human labor (hence, the increasing interest in robotization today). As long as slavery existed it hindered the use of machinery in production. The availability of cheap labor was a disincentive for the introduction of machines, which were usually more expensive than slave labor. Once slavery was eliminated, competition—an essential of the capitalist mode of production—became the driving force behind innovative mechanization and, thus, increased productivity.[22]

While Marx and Engels certainly praised the gains that capitalism engendered, they were not, as Robinson claims, blind to its contradictions or retrogressive features. They said, in fact, that this was one of its necessary consequences, what Marx termed the general law of capitalist accumulation. "It makes an accumulation of misery a necessary condition, corresponding to the accumulation of wealth. Accumulation of wealth at one pole is, therefore, at the same time accumulation of misery, the torment of labor, slavery, ignorance, brutalization and moral degradation at the opposite pole, i.e., on the side of the class that produces its own product as capital."[23] This was the context in which Marx explained the tendency of capitalism to relegate increasing numbers of workers to the unemployment lines, that is, the industrial reserve army. (If ever there was confirmation of this tendency, it clearly is seen in the historical trend of Black unemployment in the United States.)

It is not difficult, then, to understand why precapitalist ideologies like racism not only continue but flourish under bourgeois rule. Racism is a convenient means for expanding the industrial reserve army and justifying its existence. At the international level it is used in a similar way in relation to the impoverishment of the third world. Sexism, which is part of not only Europe's cultural legacy, is also employed by the bourgeoisie for such reasons and with equally devastating results.

What is most important in understanding how Marx and Engels looked at the pluses and minuses of bourgeois society—something Robinson misses—is their recognition that whatever gains workers and other oppressed obtain come only through their efforts and not the good will of capitalists.

A major element in Robinson's thesis is that Marx and Engels failed to see that Europe's proletariat bought into its racist legacy and that its revolutionary potential was, thus, undermined. This is clearly a misrepresentation in view of what both wrote and advocated on the Irish question and the slavery issue in the United States. Writing in 1870, Marx said:

> Every industrial and commercial centre in England now possesses a working class divided into two *hostile* camps, English proletarians and Irish proletarians. The ordinary English worker hates the Irish worker as a competitor who lowers his standard of life. In relation to the Irish worker, he regards himself as a member of the *ruling* nation and consequently he becomes a tool of the English aristocrats and capitalists *against Ireland,* thus strengthening their domination *over himself.* He cherishes religious, social, and national prejudices against the Irish worker. His attitude towards him is much the same as that of the "poor whites" to the Negroes in the former slave states of the USA[24] (Italics in original).

Marx indeed did recognize that racism had infected the working class and was an obstacle to its own liberation. Does this mean that he was in error in his earlier analysis of capitalism and the revolutionary potential of the working class?

To the contrary. The big picture that he and Engels presented in the *Manifesto* and elsewhere is by and large confirmed by the actual course of capitalist development and the anti-capitalist struggle in the twentieth century.

The fact is that, however much the bourgeoisie may try to perpetuate ethnic and racial identities to its advantage, the historic trend, as a result of the capitalist mode of production and despite the unevenness of this process, has been the creation of broader group ties that coincide with class. Nationalism, in fact, a key component in the bourgeois revolutions, was a step in this process beyond the parochialisms of feudal society. South Africa provides an excellent illustration of this tendency within the Black community in spite of efforts of the ruling class to the contrary. Compared to the nineteenth century, who can deny that today there is more international class consciousness for workers as well as the bourgeoisie.

Aside from the historical trend there is also what Marx and Engels termed the objective needs of the working class. In their effort to combat the prejudices of the English proletariat on the Irish question they explained its importance to their comrades in this way:

> [I]t is the task of the International everywhere to put the conflict between England and Ireland in the foreground, and everywhere to side openly with Ireland. It is the special task of the Central Council in London to make the English workers realise that *for them* the *national emancipation of Ireland* is not a question of abstract justice or humanitarian sentiment but *the first condition of their own social emancipation.*[25] (Italics in original.)

In other words, international class solidarity is the prerequisite for the liberation of the proletariat in the advanced capitalist countries as well as those in the colonial and semicolonial world. Unless the former identify with the national struggles of the oppressed and colonized they undermine their own freedom. This in a sense is a negative proof of what Marx and Engels argued. (The Malvinas/Falkland Island issue and the Irish question today offer illustrations of this proof. To the extent that English workers rally behind the Thatcher government's colonial policies in both places, they provide her the political support she needs to carry out her anti-working-class domestic policies.)

There is another side to the larger historical view of Marx and Engels that is also verified by the reality of the revolutionary process in the twentieth century. That is, revolutions in the periphery will only be secure when capitalism is eliminated in the center. In other words, the future of the worker-peasant-led struggles in the third world are dependent in the long run on the proletariat in the advanced capitalist countries. Southern Africa illustrates how this fact operates at the regional level. As a subimperialist power South Africa will continue to be an immediate threat to revolutionary struggles in the region until its working class (overwhelmingly Black) takes state power. This, it seems, is the major lesson of the recent South Africa-Mozambique security pact (the Nkomati Accord).

In his critique of Marx and Engels, Robinson's tendency is to argue against straw men of his own making. On no issue is this more apparent than the national question and its relationship to the anticolonial struggle. In a number of instances, he quotes them to show that they were aware of some of the problems in the big picture. For example, on the Irish question Marx wrote:

> For a long time I believed that it would be possible to overthrow the Irish regime by English working-class ascendancy. I have always expressed this point of view in the *New York Tribune.* Deeper study has now convinced me of the opposite. The English working class will *never accomplish anything* until it has got rid of Ireland. The lever must be applied in Ireland. That is why the Irish question is so important for the social movement in general.[26] (Italics in original.)

Can Robinson rightly criticize Marx and Engels for what they themselves acknowledged were inadequacies in their larger view? As materialists they were compelled to test their views against reality and make the necessary adjustments. As Engels once wrote, "Communism is not a doctrine but a *movement;* it proceeds not from principles but from *facts*" (italics in original).[27]

Robinson also accuses Marx and Engels of underestimating the significance of the anti-imperialist and anticolonial struggle. This is obviously not true as their above-quoted views on the Irish question make clear. What Robinson is really accusing them of is ignoring what were still in the nineteenth century relatively infrequent occurrences—third world anticolonial struggles.[28] When such movements appeared and when Marx and Engels had some familiarity with them, they generally expressed support for them.[29] This was particularly true for the Taiping Rebellion in China and Indian revolt in the 1850s. They not only sided with these struggles but made clear, contrary to Robinson's claim, that they were as important, if not more so, as the class struggle in Western Europe. In the case of the China uprising, Marx even speculated that it might spark revolutionary upheavals in Europe.[30] These ideas were to be the basis for Lenin's views on the national question, contrary to Robinson's suggestion that he had to break with Marx and Engels on this issue. Much of what Robinson employs as evidence to substantiate the reality of a Black radical tradition is the long tradition of slave revolts in the diaspora. He charges that Marx and Engels ignored or treated such struggles as insignificant.

Evidently, Robinson regards as unimportant the opening lines of the *Manifesto:* "The history of all hitherto existing society is the history of class struggle." Slave revolts were as significant for Marx as the revolt of workers. This is why he could write in 1860: "In my opinion, the biggest things that are happening in the world today are on the one hand the movement of slaves in America, started by the death of John Brown, and on the other hand the movement of the slaves in Russia."[31] Marx and Engels followed the U.S. Civil War very closely. They advocated that the North arm slaves to fight against the South and, most significantly, they had an active role through the International Workingmen's Association (First International) in the opposition of English workers to the British government's support for the South.[32] Their German followers in the United States played an important role in opposing slavery in states like Missouri.[33] Another one of Robinson's straw men is his claim that the positions of those who posed as followers of Marx and Engels reflected their actual views. Such an example is the social democratic Second International and its policies on the colonial question since the end of the nineteenth century. Almost invariably the parties of this organization either supported or acquiesced in the colonial policies of their home governments. Are Marx and Engels, who severely criticized colonialism, to be blamed for this? It was precisely because social democracy defaulted on the colonial question that Lenin, drawing on what Marx and Engels advocated, excoriated the Second International and eventually broke with it and formed the Third or Communist International.[34]

The colonial question is related to another one of Robinson's straw men. This concerns the progressive side of bourgeois political hegemony. It is the major issue he focuses on in his discussion of the ideas of W. E. B. Du Bois in his seminal work *Black Reconstruction.* Robinson supports Du Bois's analysis of post-Civil War America, which argues that bourgeois rule was not progressive and, in fact, was irrelevant for the revolutionary struggle to overthrow the slavocracy.[35]

Just as Marx and Engels recognized that the material advances brought by capitalism entailed increasing misery, they understood that bourgeois rule was also a mixed bag. This was the major lesson for them of the 1848 revolutions in Europe, which occurred about six months after Marx [and Engels] wrote the *Manifesto.* (In fact, in days of its publication.) The events revealed that the bourgeoisie would begin to default from its historically progressive role of overthrowing precapitalist political and economic forms. It was as if the bourgeoisie in its fight against the *ancien regime* began to look over its shoulder at the then barely visible, newly born class, the proletariat. The more it focused on this class the less it looked at feudalism, eventually to the point that the bourgeoisie found themselves in league with representatives of the old order. It became increasingly apparent that the tasks carried out by the bourgeoisie in earlier revolutions would have to be executed by this new class. As Marx remarked in the *Eighteenth Brumaire,* the revolution would not stop at the bourgeois phase but would be permanent, that is, socialism would now be on the agenda.

This is the framework they employed in analyzing revolutionary upheavals. Their anxiety over the U.S. Civil War, that is, whether the bourgeoisie under Lincoln's leadership would actually press the struggle to overthrow slavery, reflected this assessment of the bourgeoisie in the aftermath of 1848. They even suspected that after the War, the bourgeoisie would not grant full equality to Blacks.[36] While the verdict was still not in on the American bourgeoisie (at the time they were most familiar with the U.S. situation), they had no doubt that the European bourgeoisie had forfeited whatever redeeming features it once had.

Contrary to what Robinson says, Lenin was able to successfully lead the Russian Revolution because he had absorbed these lessons from Marx and Engels. Lenin had even committed to memory their famous *Address to the Central Authority of 1850,* which charted a revolutionary political course based on these lessons.[37]

In discussing Du Bois, Robinson quotes him on the limitations of the left in the United States, particularly the Communist Party, because of its failure to fully understand the Black struggle and the depths of racism. Du Bois's criticisms of the CP are not unique. In fact, what is a common thread (with the three figures that Robinson forefronts) is their negative experiences with Stalinism on the Black question and other issues. Du Bois apparently reconciled his differences with Stalinism since he joined the CP in 1961 and remained a member until his death two years later. Richard Wright was a member from 1934 to 1942. His espousal of Black nationalism and discomfort with the bureaucratic character of the Party put him at odds with it and eventually led to his break. Unlike the CPs of Western Europe, the American Party has more consistently followed the political line emanating from Moscow.

Although he was never affiliated with a pro-Moscow CP, C. L. R. James was also affected by Stalinism. As a Trotskyist, a member of the American Socialist Workers Party until 1951, James, of course, rejected the basic tenets of Stalinism such as socialism in one country and the Popular Front policy. However, he later broke with Trotsky over the latter's analysis of the Soviet Union; he also had differences over the Leninist conception of the revolutionary party.

In employing these three figures to argue his thesis, Robinson implies, especially in the case of Wright and Du Bois, that Stalinism is Marxism and/or Marxist-Leninism. This is a favorite incantation of the right wing and some social democratic critics of Marxist-Leninism. This is not the place to address the incorrectness of such views. It would be useful though to look at this claim in relation to the Black struggle and, more specifically, the Black radical tradition—what Robinson says these three had to turn to owing to the inadequacies of Marxism.

Firstly, what does Robinson mean by the Black radical

tradition? This is not very clear. Central to it, he claims—based on limited evidence—is the "Absence of mass violence" whether in Africa or the diaspora. To the extent that violence occurred it was turned inward because the external or material was unimportant. "[I]ts epistemology granted supremacy to metaphysics not the material."[38] The continuation of this tradition is "the ability to conserve their native consciousness of the world from alien intrusion, the ability to imaginatively recreate a precedent metaphysic while being subjected to enslavement, racial domination and repression."[39]

Aside from the fact that Robinson offers little evidence for this view—especially his generalizations about the African origins of this tradition—it appears that this tradition is not significantly different from that of other peoples, particularly those in precapitalist settings.

When Robinson applies this perspective to his three cases, what he really means is that they looked at the revolutionary process through the eyes of Blacks and assigned a leading role in it to the Black masses. The above discussion on the national question has hopefully laid to rest Robinson's claim that Marx and Engels had little relevance to the Black struggle—at least during their lifetime. Lenin's views on the national question and Blacks, which had their roots in Marx and Engels, were appreciated by Du Bois, Wright, and James.

Trotsky, whose position on the national question was similar to that of Lenin, was able to analyze developments in the Black struggle between the two world wars. The political tendency that James led inside the SWP from 1940 to 1947 said this about Trotsky's views:

> One of Trotsky's greatest contributions to the American party was his insistence for over ten years on the need to adapt the Leninist

> policy on the national question to the Negro problem in the United States . . . The Negro question is part of the national question in the Marxist sense of the term . . . Lenin and Trotsky and the early Communist International made invaluable contributions to this question that are indispensable for the arming of the party . . .[40]

Although he differed with Trotsky on other issues, James has never recanted this view. Contrary to what Robinson suggests, James clearly did not regard Marxism to be irrelevant to Black liberation.

As for Robinson's claim that Marxists are equivocal about Black self-determination, it should be noted that in a discussion with James in 1939 Trotsky mildly rebuked him for deprecating Black nationalism and argued, in opposition to James, that Marcus Garvey's movement was progressive.[41]

Trotsky made a number of other points:

> The Negroes are not yet awakened and they are not yet united with the white workers. 99.9 per cent of the American workers are chauvinists, in relation to the Negroes they are hangmen . . . It is necessary to teach the American beasts . . . Those American workers who say: "The Negroes should separate when they so desire and we will defend them against our American police"—these are revolutionaries. . . . The argument that the slogan for "self-determination" leads away from the class basis is an adaptation to the ideology of the white workers. . . . It is possible . . . that the Negroes will become the most advanced section [in the radicalization of the working class] . . . They will furnish the vanguard. I am absolutely sure that they will in any case fight better than the white workers.[42]

It would be difficult to conclude that Trotsky's opinions were incompatible with those of the three individuals that Robinson describes. As in the case of Lenin, they had their origins in Marx and Engels. Stalin's policies, on the other hand, had little in common with this tradition. What has always been central to the Stalinist position on the national question—in the United States and elsewhere—is the subordination of the interest of oppressed nationalities to those of the Soviet bureaucracy. To suggest, as Robinson does, that this is Marxist-Leninism is to erect another straw man.

James's differences with Trotsky centered on his positions that the Soviet revolution had degenerated into a state capitalist regime and that a Leninist vanguard party was not necessary for making a revolution. The question is, why should these views constitute an example of the Black radical tradition as Robinson suggests? Whites, both on the left and right, have had similar positions. The problem is the conceptual weakness that Robinson has not adequately resolved.

A major shortcoming with Robinson's thesis is that he himself falls victim to what he erroneously accuses Marx and Engels of, the formulation of a perspective that inadequately addresses historical reality. It is Robinson, with his static idealist methodology, that has difficulty in dealing with new situations. How else can one explain his virtual ignoring of the actual course of third world struggles and the Black liberation movement, in particular, since the years when James, Du Bois, and Wright were politically active? (At most he spends about three pages making superficial and sometimes mistaken comments about such events.) For a work that purports to unearth and trace the development of the Black radical tradition, it is noteworthy that Robinson does not even mention the Grenada revolution.

An example of a work that has a completely opposite orientation is A. M. Babu's above mentioned *African Socialism or Socialist*

Africa? Babu, an active participant in the Black struggle—that more than anything probably explains the differences—has essentially drawn up a balance sheet of the African revolution for the last twenty years. Unlike Robinson, he concludes that what is needed throughout Africa are revolutionary parties armed with a Marxist-Leninist program. Babu devotes a major portion of his analysis to critique what is Robinson's key contention, that is, class analysis is irrelevant to the Black struggle.

It is not enough to assert the existence of a Black radical tradition as Robinson does. The key question is its relevance as a program of struggle for Black people today. If Robinson operated in a materialist framework, he might be interested in which perspectives in the Black radical tradition have stood up against the test of time, that is, relate to the actual changes in the Black nation and the third world and the entire international situation. For example, if the Cubans had adhered to James's analysis of the Soviet Union as a state capitalist regime, it is doubtful that they could have consolidated their revolution. Armed with his perspective, they would probably have dismissed the USSR as a likely ally.

To follow Robinson's argument that Marx's notion of a revolutionary proletariat is obsolete is to pursue a course that contradicts the living reality of revolutionary struggles in places like Nicaragua, El Salvador, South Africa, and Grenada (until October 1983). While Robinson may have written off the proletariat in the advanced capitalist countries, revolutionaries in Central America and the Caribbean have certainly not. They have increasingly taken steps to appeal to the class interests of American workers, and in most instances where they have been able to break through the bourgeois ideological fence that envelops most U.S. workers they have gotten a favorable response.[43] Finally, Robinson might consider what the late Maurice Bishop said in an interview in Grenada in July 1980.

> Let me add just one final thing. That is to say that we, without intending to be disrespectful, would very strongly recommend to the Black movement in America the importance of developing the firmest and closest links with the white working-class movement and the white progressive movement. Our feeling certainly is that in order to win that struggle inside of America, it's extremely important that all progressive forces get together and wage a consistent fight against the real enemy.[44]

As Black people each of us has an obligation to ponder the advice of Bishop who led what this reviewer considers to have been the highest expression so far of the Black radical tradition.

"cc"

3

The Eurocentric Marx and Engels and Other Related Myths

Introduction to My Essay in *Marxism, Modernity and Postcolonial Studies*[1]

CENTRAL TO CEDRIC ROBINSON'S CRITIQUE of Marx and Engels's project is the charge of Eurocentrism. Thus, by implication, a project that didn't speak to the reality of the non-European world majority, its African component specifically. In my 1985 review, I addressed that claim mainly by saying that many third world revolutionaries thought otherwise. An obviously important response, but it failed to say how Marx and Engels might have responded to the charge.

No longer a member of the Socialist Workers Party (SWP) after 1995, I had a lot of time to dive deeply into the writings of Marx and Engels, specifically, what the SWP educational project had introduced me to: the fifty-volume English language *Marx-Engels Collected Works* (MECW). With the collapse of the Soviet Union and its nearby sister regimes, I decided that it would be an opportune moment to make the case for Marx and Engels's democratic credentials. Moscow and its partisans elsewhere no longer held the authority for how to read the project that the two communists helped birth. My 2000 *Marx and Engels: Their Contribution to the Democratic Breakthrough* was the first book product of that plunge into the MECW. In it I argued that no two individuals contributed more to the democratic quest than Marx and Engels: first, owing to their being, first and foremost, not thinkers, as Robinson claimed, but rather political activists; second, owing to their prioritization of the proletariat, class society's most efficacious democrats.

Robinson's *Black Marxism* continued to weigh on my brain as I read and perused those all-so-rich Marx-Engels volumes. Along the way, I noted or remembered—or, at least, tried to—facts that contradicted his Eurocentric charge. When the opportunity presented itself to write something about what I learned on the topic, I jumped on it. Thus, my contribution to *Marxism, Modernity and Postcolonial Studies*, a collection published in 2002, one of the first that questioned *en vogue* postmodern orthodoxy about the Marxist project, the real one. Two cases elaborated in the essay, the Irish question and the U.S. Civil War, were anticipated but only briefly in my 1985 review. It's the Russian case, as the reader will see, on which I rested my rejection of the Eurocentric charge. Except for its most unreconstructed skin-color wing, Black nationalists rightly exempted Russia, once an overwhelmingly peasant country of rainbow skin colors, from Western Europe. Reproduced here is the original publication with just a few stylistic tweaks and updated notes.

The Eurocentric Marx and Engels and Other Related Myths

Europe's failed revolutions of 1848 and 1849 were followed by a decade-long lull in the class struggle. Karl Marx and Frederick

Engels, like others who had been brought into active politics during those two momentous years, were always on the lookout for new revolutionary initiatives—a posture that could sometimes lead to wishful thinking. When developments in Russia at the end of 1858 suggested that the revival might begin there and then spread to Western Europe, Marx, writing from London to his comrade in Manchester, advised caution this time. Given capitalism's still ascendant trajectory in other areas of the world, such a revival might "be crushed in this little corner of the earth."[2] The fate of the revolutionary process in Western Europe was not only dependent now on developments elsewhere but its own weight in that process had diminished. Contrary, then, to what has come to be a staple in much of the literature, Marx and Engels, at least by 1859, had begun to look beyond the "little corner" in which they lived to the rest of the world for revolutionary initiatives.

This article disputes the charge that Marx and Engels were Eurocentric—a charge that has roots in the long-established Marxological enterprise and has since been embraced by postcolonialists and postmodernists to varying degrees—and argues that they were first and foremost revolutionaries who viewed the entire globe as their theater of operations. To make my case I begin by showing how the Marx-Engels partnership began with a global perspective and then, when presented with new political opportunities in the aftermath of the post-1848–1849 lull, sought to realize their vision. Along the way I challenge two related myths: "England as the model" and "Marx against the peasantry." Rather than England, I argue that they looked increasingly, certainly after 1870, to Russia as the revolutionary vanguard, an overwhelmingly peasant country that had only one foot in Europe and not the Europe that the Eurocentric charge refers to, that is, its most developed western flank. Lastly, I speculate briefly about what they might say about today's political reality.

Communism: A "World-Historical" Process

Long before 1858, Marx and Engels had looked beyond their "little corner" in explaining and making political judgments about the revolutionary process. Though Hegel's philosophy of world history no doubt prepared them to think globally, it was when they became conscious communists and formed their revolutionary partnership in 1844 that they concretized their own position. In *The German Ideology*, where they presented for the first time their "new world view," i.e., the "materialist conception of history," they argued that only with the "universal development of productive forces" would it be possible for "a *universal* intercourse between men [to be] established . . . making each nation dependent on the revolution of others, and finally [putting] *world-historical*, empirically universal individuals in place of local ones." Thus "communism . . . can only have a 'world-historical' existence."[3] Shortly afterward, this and other fundamental premises of their new perspective would find their way into the *Manifesto of the Communist Party*. The draft from which Marx worked, Engels's catechized "Principles of Communism," was more explicit. To the question, "Will it be possible for this revolution to take place in one country alone?" the reply is "No. . . . It is a worldwide revolution and will therefore be worldwide in scope."[4] Written on the eve of the 1848–1849 revolutions, Marx and Engels clearly understood that only the "real movement" could provide the actual answer to the question. Nevertheless, the global orientation with which they entered those upheavals served as their frame of reference in making political assessments along the way.

Within a couple of weeks of the *Manifesto*'s publication, the long-anticipated revolutions of 1848–1849 began. For present purposes, the most significant aspect of Marx and Engels's very rich and instructive practice in those events over the course of fifteen months is that they gave active support to national liberation struggles, particularly those of the Poles, Hungarians, and Italians. By the end of 1848, they had concluded that the fate of the German revolution was linked to the successful outcome of a worldwide revolutionary process that combined national liberation, anti-feudal and anti-capitalist struggles "waged in Canada as in Italy, in East Indies as in Prussia, in Africa as on the Danube."[5] In the relative calm of London and the British Museum in 1849–1850, they undertook research that allowed them to strengthen this judgment. Their findings made clear that the world's economic center had by then shifted from Western Europe to the United States. "The most important thing to have occurred [in America], more important even than the February [1848] Revolution, is the discovery of the California gold-mines. . . . [As a result the] centre of gravity of world commerce, Italy in the Middle Ages, England in modern times, is now the southern half of the North American peninsula. . . . The Pacific Ocean will have the same role as the Atlantic has now and the Mediterranean had in antiquity and in the Middle Ages—that of the great water highway of world commerce."[6]

This assessment, apparently the first ever made,[7] would have predicted further revolutionary implications for the peoples of Asia, especially the Chinese. News of the Taiping Rebellion in 1850, the result in part of British commercial penetration into coastal areas, suggested that "the oldest and least perturbable kingdom on earth [was on] the eve of a social upheaval, which, in any event, is bound to have the most significant results for civilisation."[8] Marx and Engels could barely conceal their joy about the possibility of a bourgeois democratic revolution in China and the world-shaking repercussions it would have. If Western Europe had once been at the center of their worldview, this was certainly no longer true after 1850. Their global orientation allowed them to see clearly beyond "this little corner of the earth" without a hint of nostalgia.

Marx and Engels's practice during the revolutions reveals their actual position on the peasant question. When the first revolutionary outbreak occurred in Germany in March 1848, they quickly supplemented the *Manifesto* with an addendum that addressed the issue explicitly. (The *Manifesto*'s failure to cover this subject is often taken to justify the widely held misperception that they discounted the peasantry.)[9] The oft-ignored document, the *Demands of the Communist Party of Germany*, basically a program for a bourgeois democratic revolution in Germany, spoke to the immediate needs of the peasantry—an ending of all feudal obligations and a radical land reform. The program informed Marx and Engels's practice throughout the course of their involvement in the upheavals, especially their ceaseless—but in the end unsuccessful—efforts to forge a worker-peasant alliance. This perspective forever informed their revolutionary strategy and tactics, especially for countries in which the social and political weight of the peasantry was decisive.[10] During the Paris Commune in 1871 (about which I shall have more to say later), for example, Marx did all he could from afar to convince its leadership that the insurgency's survival depended on getting the support of the peasantry. After his death, it fell to Engels in 1894 to write the most comprehensive programmatic statement they ever produced on the subject, *The Peasant Question in France and Germany*.

The failure of the 1848 revolutions allowed Marx and Engels to give more detailed attention to developments beyond Europe. Three settings are instructive for our purposes here: Algeria, India, and Mexico. Regarding the first, a month before the *Manifesto* was published Engels applauded the French conquest of Algeria and defeat of the uprising led by the religious leader Abd el-Kader, saying that it was "an important and fortunate fact for the progress of civilization."[11] Nine years later in 1857 he had completely reversed his stance and now severely denounced French colonial rule and expressed sympathy for religious-led Arab resistance to the imperial power.[12] Their historical materialist perspective explains Engels's initial position. However, the real movement of history, especially the lessons of 1848, had taught that however progressive French imperialism may have been prior to then it had outworn its usefulness; the opposition of the colonial subjects was now the movement to be supported. Shortly before his death in 1883, Marx visited Algeria in the hope that its climate would improve his health. A comment to his daughter Laura about the situation of the colonized reveals that his identification with them as fellow fighters had not waned: "They will go to rack and ruin without a revolutionary movement."[13]

Marx's first sustained writing on India strikes a similar tone to that sounded by Engels about Algeria in 1848. He described in 1853 England's undermining of local industries and social structures as "causing a social revolution," however "sickening . . . it must be to human feeling to witness" the effects of such policies.[14] But by the time of the Sepoy Mutiny against British rule in 1857–1859, Marx and Engels's sympathy for the anticolonial struggle was unquestionable. As Marx told his partner: "In view of the Drain of Men and Bullion which she will cost the English, India is now our best ally."[15] For both of them, therefore, the uprisings in these countries were exactly what Marx had forecast at the end of 1848 about the global interdependency of the revolutionary movement. Later in 1871, the International Working Men's Association (IWMA), which Marx effectively headed, reported that a request had come to it from Calcutta to establish a branch of the body in the city. The secretary for the organization's executive committee in London, the General Council, "was instructed . . . to urge the necessity of enrolling natives in the Association," thus making clear that the new affiliate was not to be an exclusively expatriate branch.[16]

Finally, there is the case of Mexico. For Engels in 1849, the U.S. conquest of northern Mexico was "waged wholly and solely in the interest of civilisation," particularly because the "energetic Yankees"—unlike the "lazy Mexicans"—would bring about the "rapid exploitation of the California gold mines" and, hence, for the "third time in history give world trade a new direction."[17] Subsequent history and research forced them to qualify this assessment. With the U.S. Civil War looming, Marx wrote in 1861 that in "the foreign, as in domestic, policy of the United States, the interests of the slaveholders served as the guiding star." The seizure of northern Mexico had in fact made it possible to "impose slavery and with it the rule of the slaveholders" not only in Texas but later in present-day New Mexico and Arizona .[18] The benefits that came with California were compromised by the "barbarity" of slavery's extension.

One of the alleged problems with Marxism and one to which Marx himself succumbed, according to Stuart Hall, is its "Eurocentric take" on the "origins of capitalism as organically growing out of feudalism . . . peacefully evolving out of the womb of feudalism." This view, says Hall, is belied by the experiences of anyone "from anywhere in the periphery of the capitalist system."[19] For Hall, of course, the problem is symptomatic of the limitations of what he and others often call "classical Marxism"—in this instance, apparently, that "Marx took [England] as his paradigm case in *Capital*."[20] While it is not exactly clear what Hall is getting at, he seems to suggest that however "peaceful" the European origins of capitalism might have been, this was definitely not the case with what would later be called the periphery.

This is an odd criticism since Hall certainly knows what Marx wrote in *Capital* about the emergence of capitalism in the center, especially England, let alone the periphery: Marx's chapter, "The Genesis of the Industrial Capitalist," with its famous last sentence, "Capital comes [into the world] dripping from head to toe, from every pore, with blood and dirt," indicted a process that was no less horrible in the center than in the periphery.

A New Revolutionary Era

From their global posture, Marx and Engels were predisposed to look for revolutionary initiatives beyond Western Europe. Hence, they concluded in the beginning of 1863 that "the era of revolution has now fairly opened in Europe once more."[21] The basis for this judgment was the peasant uprising in Poland that year; thus "the lava will flow from East to West." However, even before then, other signs had already appeared on the political horizon that gave cause for optimism. At the beginning of 1860, Marx declared that "the most momentous thing happening in the world today is the slave movement—on the one hand, in America, started by the death of Brown, and in Russia, on the other."[22] He was referring, of course, to the abortive rebellion of the abolitionist John Brown at Harpers Ferry, Virginia, a few months earlier, which in turn had stimulated at least one slave uprising in its aftermath. As for Russia—the "lava from the East"—its "slaves," i.e., serfs, had since 1858 also been on the march for emancipation. A year later, in a move to preempt a revolt from below, the tsar abolished serfdom. Because Marx and Engels viewed the class struggle globally they gave more weight to the conjuncture of struggles in various countries than to isolated ones. The fight against slavery and other pre-capitalist modes of exploitation was obviously key in labor's struggle against capital. In his preface to *Capital*, written seven years later and after the U.S. Civil War, Marx would be even more explicit: "As in the 18th century, the American War of Independence sounded the tocsin for the European middle class, so in the 19th century, the American Civil War sounded it for the European working class." Political reality had revealed by 1867 that, of the two "slave movements" in 1860, the one on the other side of the Atlantic was more decisive. Six decades later, however, in 1917, "the lava [would] flow from East to West."

With the determination that a new revolutionary era had opened, Marx and Engels were primed to return to active politics when the opportunity presented itself. In 1864, at an international meeting of trade unionists in London, Marx was invited to represent the German movement, and soon emerged as the guiding force in what came to be called the International Working Men's Association, or First International—the first truly international proletarian organization. Though the International's influence and legacy was enormous, it came to an effective end in 1873. A major reason was ruling-class attacks against it for its well-known support, with Marx leading the way, of the Paris Commune of 1871. An important casualty of this campaign was the participation of English trade union officials in the organization's leadership body, the General Council, based in London. Their departure is instructive and reveals how Marx and Engels reassessed the revolutionary potential of the English working class.

More than a year before the Paris Commune, Marx commented to Engels on the prospects for revolution: "I am firmly convinced that although the first blow will come from France, Germany is far riper for a social movement, and will grow far over the heads of the French."[23] While the "first blow" did indeed come from France in the form of the Commune, Marx and Engels were still convinced that the axis of world revolution had moved east of

Paris. Implicit in their view was a downgrading of the importance of the English movement. They indeed had once looked to the latter as the vanguard of the workers' movement owing to the advanced character of capitalism in England and the existence of a genuine workers' party, the Chartists. What explains, therefore, their reevaluation of the English movement?

As early as 1858, Engels began to have second thoughts about the revolutionary potential of England. When the Chartist leader Ernest Jones sought to maneuver with the liberal bourgeoisie by watering down the historical demands of the Chartist program, Engels wrote that it was symptomatic of "the fact that the English proletariat is actually becoming more and more bourgeois." He then offered an explanation: "In the case of a nation which exploits the entire world this is, of course, justified to some extent."[24] The booty of British imperialism had begun to compromise England's workers. It was exactly this point that Marx responded to in his comment that the revolutionary movement might be "CRUSHED in this little corner of the earth" because capitalism, with Britain in the lead, was still "ascendant" globally.

The English trade union leaders who were instrumental in the International's foundation came almost exclusively from the building trades and skilled crafts. The latter, in particular, were mainly concerned about their survival in the face of industrial capitalism. Both the building trades and skilled crafts' officialdom were motivated to participate in the IWMA on the basis of narrow economic and political interests and not proletarian internationalism.[25] In his *Inaugural Address* for the IWMA, Marx had alluded to the stratification in the English working class by noting that "a minority [had gotten] their real wages somewhat advanced" during the unprecedented expansion of British capitalism in the third quarter of the nineteenth century. The political repercussions of these differences within the working class would only become clear in the course of the IWMA's experience in England. More than anything, it was the suffrage question and electoral politics that first revealed to Marx the reality of the trade unionists' participation on the General Council (GC), specifically, their decision to bloc with British liberals—in contravention of GC policy—in the electoral arena to support household instead of universal male suffrage.

If the trade unionists on the GC had sold out the English working class on the suffrage issue, Marx made sure that they would not be able to do the same on the Irish question. His strategy was to craft a GC policy position that made it clear that the IWMA's support of the recently jailed Fenian prisoners and Irish self-determination was unequivocal while attempting, at the same time, to drive a wedge between the trade unionists and the liberal Gladstone government. If Marx's resolution on the Irish question was difficult for the trade unionists to swallow, his now famous homage to the Communards, *Civil War in France,* proved to be indigestible. Their disagreement with its line forced those who were still formally members of the GC to completely sever their ties with the IWMA. Under pressure from their liberal allies they chose to distance themselves from the fallen Communards and Marx's uncompromising defense of them. Whatever hopes, therefore, Marx and Engels had once pinned on the English movement had clearly been dispelled by the reaction of their leaders to the demise of the Commune.

At The Hague in 1872, effectively the last congress of the IWMA, Marx left little doubt about what he thought of the trade union leaders. When one of them questioned the credentials of one of the delegates with the charge that he didn't represent English workers, Marx retorted: "It does credit to [him] that he is not one of the so-called leaders of the English workers, since these men are more or less bribed by the bourgeoisie and the government."[26] Although his widely publicized remarks led to a complete rupture with the reformists, Marx was still unapologetic two years later: "I knew that I was letting myself in for unpopularity, slander, etc., but such consequences have always been a matter of indifference to me. Here and there people are beginning to see that in making that denunciation I was only doing my duty."[27]

In an analysis of the parliamentary elections in 1874, Engels returned to the point that he and Marx had raised in 1858 to explain the political backwardness of English workers. "This is understandable in a country in which the working class has shared more than anywhere else in the advantages of the immense expansion of its large-scale industry. Nor could it have been otherwise in an England that rules the world market."[28] While politics was also determinant—the willingness of the ruling class to grant the historical demands of the Chartists was particularly important—the impact of imperialism on the consciousness of English workers was still, for Engels as late as 1883, decisive. "Participation in the domination of the world market was and is the economic basis of the English workers' political nullity."[29] Only when the world monopoly of Britain's rulers would be challenged by competitors, with the resulting diminution of the booty, would English workers begin to move. Contrary, therefore, to the standard Marxological portrait, Marx and Engels had long abandoned—at least by 1871—their earlier optimism about the exemplary role of English workers.

In no place was the reality of British imperialism and its domestic repercussions clearer than in its continuing subjugation of the Irish people. Marx's comment in 1869 that the "English working class . . . will never be able to do anything decisive here in England before they separate their attitude towards Ireland . . . from that of the ruling classes"[30] is as relevant today as then. The comment represented a key shift in his and Engels's strategy for the Irish movement for self-determination. Prior to then, they had held that the overthrow of capital in England was the precondition for Ireland's liberation. Implicit in this stance was the assumption that the Irish struggle should take its lead from that of the English workers. But the initiatives taken by the Fenians in 1867 forced them to reconsider this assessment.

The relegation of Ireland to a giant farm to meet England's food needs was the fundamental reason for the revision Marx made in his political stance; the process gave England's landlord class a new lease on life with all the resulting negative social and political effects—in effect, the first detailed analysis of a process that would be generalized throughout the world, the phenomenon of underdevelopment. It was in response to the landlordism factor, more than any other, that Marx would write to Engels in 1869: "The lever must be applied in Ireland." As he observed: "Quite apart from international justice, it is a *precondition to the emancipation of the English working class* to transform the present *forced union* (i.e., the enslavement of Ireland) into *equal and free confederation*, if possible, into *complete separation* if need be."[31] This revised view became the basis for the positions the GC took on the amnesty campaign for the Fenian prisoners that year.

The Russians in the Vanguard

Just as Marx and Engels were concluding that the English working class was not "the model" they were beginning, not coincidentally, to look further eastward—to Russia. Proposing in 1863 that a new revolutionary era had begun, they pointed to the peasant movement then underway in Polish Russia. But it would take about seven years before they made direct contact with Russia's nascent revolutionary movement. In the meantime, and symptomatic of developments there, revolutionaries in Moscow took the initiative in 1872 to have *Capital* published in Russian, its first translation into another language.

To gain a better appreciation of Russia's importance, Marx began in early 1870 to learn Russian. "He has begun," according to his wife, "studying Russian as if it were a matter of life and death."[32] After reading *The Condition of the Working Class in Russia* by N. Flerovsky, the Russian Narodnik socialist—a work that Marx described to Engels as "the most important book published since your work on the *Condition of the Working Class*,[33] one feels deeply convinced that a most terrible social revolution . . . is irrepressible in Russia and near at hand. This is good news. Russia and England are the two great pillars of the present European system. All the rest is of secondary importance, even *la belle France et la savante Allemagne*."[34] Five years later, Engels accurately foresaw—though it would clearly take longer than he expected—that the social revolution in Russia would "have inevitable repercussions on Germany."[35] From this point to the very end of their lives, both Marx and Engels prioritized developments in Russia, a fact ignored by almost all Marxologists.

Due in part to the enormous impact that *Capital* had in Russia—the Russian edition sold better than any other—as well as his renown in connection with the IWMA, Marx was asked in March 1870 by a group of Russian émigrés in Geneva to represent them on the GC in the IWMA, thus beginning his formal links with the generation of Russian revolutionaries from whom the leadership of 1917 would emerge. It's instructive to note that the Geneva exiles wanted Marx to be their representative because "the practical character of the movement was so similar in Germany and Russia, [and] the writings of Marx were so generally known and appreciated by the Russian youth."[36] Although the standard charge is that Marx and Engels's perspective did not address the reality of underdeveloped settings such as Russia, radicalizing Russian youth in the 1870s saw otherwise. They sought out his views on the prospects and course of socialist revolution in their homeland. Specifically, would Russia have to undergo a prolonged stage of capitalist development or could it proceed directly to socialist transformation on the basis of communal property relations that prevailed in much of the countryside at that time?

Exactly because of the socioeconomic changes that Russia was then undergoing, Marx was reluctant to make any categorical judgments. It was in his letter to a group of Russian revolutionary democrats in 1877 that he made his oft-cited warning against turning his "historical sketch of the genesis of capitalism in Western Europe [in *Capital*] into a historical-philosophical theory of general development, imposed by fate on all peoples, whatever the historical circumstances in which they are placed."[37] What he was willing at that time to say about Russia was that if it "continues along the path it has followed since 1861, it will miss the finest chance that history has ever offered to a nation, only to undergo all the fatal vicissitudes of the capitalist system."[38]

When Vera Zasulich, one of the founders of the Marx party in Russia, asked Marx in 1881 whether the Russian peasant commune could survive in the face of the ever-expanding capitalist mode of production, Marx was again cautious. In order for it to be saved and become the basis for socialist property relations, "it would first be necessary to eliminate the deleterious influences which are assailing it from all sides."[39] In other words, as one of the drafts of his letter put it, "To save the Russian commune, a Russian revolution is needed."[40] The drafts upon which this reply was based went into far greater detail on the peasant question and revealed how closely Marx had been following developments in Russia, especially on rural social relations.

As for the politics and strategy of socialist revolution in Russia, it was Engels who first predicted what would be involved. Rejecting the Blanquist view that the Russian peasant was "instinctively revolutionary," he warned against "a premature attempt at insurrection," since "Russia undoubtedly is on the eve of a revolution." He provided a most accurate sketch of what did in fact occur, if significantly later than he expected:

> a growing recognition among the enlightened strata of the nation concentrated in the capital that . . . a revolution is impending, and the illusion that it will be possible to guide this revolution along a smooth constitutional channel. Here all the conditions of a revolution are combined, of a revolution that, started by the upper classes of the capital, perhaps even by the government itself, must be rapidly carried further, beyond the first constitutional phase, by the peasants, of a revolution that will be of the greatest importance for the whole of Europe.[41]

Marx saw a similar scenario, and when the Russo-Turkish War broke out in 1877, both he and Engels thought it would precipitate Russia's social revolution. They got the algebra if not the mathematics right—it would indeed be a war, the Russo-Japanese War of 1905 that would initiate the developments leading up to 1917.

Both Marx and Engels also held that the opening of the social revolution in Russia would spread westward, leading to "*radical change throughout Europe.*"[42] In fact, the "overthrow of Tsarist Russia . . . is . . . one of the first conditions of the German proletariat's ultimate triumph."[43] To a close Party member in Germany in 1882, Engels counseled that the next international should only be formed when the moment was right:

> Such events are already taking shape in Russia where the avant-garde of the revolution will be going into battle. You should—or

> so we think—wait for this and its inevitable repercussions on Germany, and then the moment will also have come for a big manifesto and the establishment of an *official*, formal International, which can, however, no longer be a propaganda association but simply an association for action.[44]

This was most prophetic, since it was indeed the Russian Revolution in 1917 that led to the formation in 1919 of the Third or Communist International which proudly proclaimed its adherence to Marx's program.

Finally, in the "Preface" to the second Russian edition of the *Manifesto* in 1882, Marx and Engels wrote that "Russia forms the vanguard of revolutionary action in Europe." To the end of his life, which was only fifteen months away, Marx continued to devote his attention to the peasant question in Russia—the same subject to which the young Lenin addressed his initial research.[45] After Marx's death, Engels continued to believe that the ingredients existed for Russia to play a vanguard role in the revolutionary process. Hence, the beginning of regular correspondence and contact with Zasulich, Georgi Plekhanov, and other leaders of the recently formed Emancipation of Labor group, the first explicitly Russian Marxist organization. As he and Marx had earlier noted, the seriousness with which the Russians took their writings was exceptional. They sought Marx's views on the key theoretical issue that he had earlier been asked to address—whether Russia could bypass capitalist development and proceed directly to socialism based on the common ownership of property of the traditional peasant commune. There were, of course, enormous political implications to this most vital question.

Engels returned to the subject of Russia in 1894, almost a decade and a half after he and Marx had last thoroughly discussed it. Russia's development in the intervening years, he observed, had been decidedly capitalist, and the "proletarianisation of a large proportion of the peasantry and the decay of the old communistic commune proceeds at an ever quickening pace." Whether enough of the traditional communes remained for a "point of departure for communistic development," Engels could not say:

> But this much is certain: if a remnant of this commune is to be preserved, the first condition is the fall of tsarist despotism—revolution in Russia. This will not only tear the great mass of the nation, the peasants, away from the isolation of their villages . . . and lead them out onto the great stage . . . it will also give the labour movement of the West fresh impetus and create new, better conditions in which to carry on the struggle, thus hastening the victory of the modern industrial proletariat, without which present-day Russia can never achieve a socialist transformation, whether proceeding from the commune or from capitalism.[46]

Thus, indisputably, and contrary to all of the future Stalinist distortions of Marx and Engels's views, Russia could "never achieve a socialist transformation" *without* the overthrow of the bourgeoisie in Western Europe by its own proletariat. Russia would not only be the "impetus" for the socialist revolution in the West, but its own revolution was also inextricably linked to that outcome. This forecast would be profoundly and tragically confirmed by subsequent history.

The Russian case reveals unequivocally, therefore, that Marx and Engels could be as programmatically at home in an overwhelmingly peasant country, characterized by extremely uneven and combined development, in transition from one mode of production to another, as in the more industrialized social formations of Western Europe—doing, in other words, everything that "classical Marxism" is incapable of doing, according to postcolonial and postmodernist critics. Such fables can persist as long as the real Marx and Engels—their writings, pronouncements, and actions in their entirety, and not just what academics or others who might have spoken in their names afterward, have designated as their canon or "classics"—are ignored.[47]

Conclusion

Engels's very prescient observation in 1894 that socialist transformation in Russia could not be achieved without the overthrow of the bourgeoisie in the advanced capitalist countries of Western Europe is worth revisiting. It was consistent with everything that he and his partner had argued from the very beginning of their endeavor: the revolutionary process is a "world-historical" event. The Russian Revolution of 1917, arguably the most influential event of the twentieth century, appears to have embodied in both its glory and agony, exactly what Engels was getting at. While it might be possible to overturn capitalist relations of production in one country, to advance beyond that point to socialist transformation required revolutionary transformation in more advanced capitalist countries. That didn't happen and therein lies the explanation for the retrogressions that increasingly unfolded in the aftermath of the 1917 revolution.[48]

The Irish case had similar lessons. In revising their view about the direction of the revolutionary process, that is, looking to the Irish nationalists rather than the English working class for initiatives, Marx and Engels were under no illusion that developments in England were irrelevant. To the contrary, the success in the long run of the Irish struggle depended on whether it got a positive hearing from the producing classes in England because it was there that the material prerequisites for an egalitarian society—the basis of real self-determination—existed. But the Irish did not have to wait for the English working class to go into action; their initiative might inspire England's working classes into revolutionary motion. It was also from this perspective that Marx and Engels viewed the insurgencies in Algeria and India.

If the twentieth century taught anything, it's that although a revolutionary initiative can more easily be undertaken in an underdeveloped than in an advanced social formation, it is less likely to be consummated in such a setting. In declaring, as they did in 1882, that "Russia forms the vanguard of revolutionary action in Europe," Marx and Engels did not assume that socialist transformation was on the immediate agenda in an underdeveloped country like Russia. Rather, the transition would begin there through the democratic revolution but could only be consummated as a socialist revolution if it spread to a more advanced capitalist country, particularly Germany. Socialist Germany could then assist Russia in its transition. Between the Russian Revolution in October 1917 and the failure of German socialists to take power in 1923—coming on the heels of two previous failed attempts—this seemed like a real possibility.

The conclusion that Marx reached at the end of 1848 about the global interdependency of the revolutionary process rings even truer now than then. It is worth repeating his declaration that only with the "universal development of productive forces" would it be possible for "a *universal* intercourse between men [to be] established . . . making each nation dependent on the revolution of others." What is so striking about the world in which we live today is exactly the "universal development of productive forces" that the much overused term "globalization" tries in part to capture. If it were true in 1858 that the success of the socialist revolution in the "little corner of the earth" in which Marx and Engels lived was inextricably linked to the revolutionary process elsewhere, it is all the more true today. Furthermore, their claim that socialist transformation could begin in the underdeveloped world, but had to extend to advanced capitalist countries to be successful, is more relevant today than ever. Evidence continues to mount that the post–Second World War third world revolutionary process, often in the name of Marxism, may have reached an impasse that can only be resolved in the advanced capitalist world—the site of the material prerequisites. That the producers of the world today have more in common with each other than at any time in their history, and can engage in "*universal* intercourse" unlike ever before, gives the final lines of the *Manifesto* a currency that they have never had: "The Proletarians have nothing to lose but their chains. They have a world to win."

4

Marx on Race: What the Critics Get Wrong

IMPLICIT IN ROBINSON'S EUROCENTRIC CHARGE about Marx's project is its failure to address that all so essential feature of the American reality—the race question and thus the need for a "Black radical tradition" to make up for that deficit. Hence, Du Bois's inclusion in Robinson's narrative despite his "irreconcilable roles—as a Black radical thinker and as a sympathetic critic of Marx."[1] But is it true that Marx and Engels had nothing to say about the race question in the United States, nor make sense of it and, therefore, had the need to rely on "their less gifted epigoni" to make up for that supposed failing? And, that Du Bois was a "critic" of their project? Both questions, particularly the first, figure prominently in my 2024 co-authored book, *The Communist and the Revolutionary Liberal in the Second American Revolution: Comparing Karl Marx and Frederick Douglass in Real-Time.*[2]

To make a credible case for Marx and Engels's democratic credentials—the subject of my 2000 book *Marx and Engels*—comparisons with the best that liberalism had to offer in real-time politics, I argued, were necessary. Comparing how Alexis de Tocqueville and the Marx-Engels team performed in the 1848–1849 revolutions, the European Spring, provided an answer. Tocqueville, author of *Democracy in America*, the evidence reveals, proved to be an unapologetic counterrevolutionary. Marx and Engels, in striking contrast, passed that crucial moment's democratic test with flying colors because they prioritized the empowerment of the only efficacious democrats in the millennia-old history of class society—the proletariat, the class Tocqueville most feared.

What about John Stuart Mill, the other outstanding liberal of the nineteenth century? Unlike his onetime friend Tocqueville, Mill, as I document in my 2019 book *Marxism versus Liberalism*, sided with the Marx-Engels team in being on the right side of history when it came to the next most important moment in the democratic quest after the European Spring—the U.S. Civil War. But Mill, unlike Marx, never pretended to be the activist, willing to put in the requisite time and energy needed to advance the Union cause and destroy the reprehensible institution of chattel slavery—the key obstacle in that moment to the democratic quest. For that reason, I decided that Frederick Douglass would be the appropriate nineteenth-century liberal for a comparison with Marx, particularly when it came to the Civil War.

The Communist and the Revolutionary Liberal required a deeper dive into the *Marx-Engels Collected Works* (MECW) regarding the class-versus-race question. The history-making events of the Civil War and its outcome posed questions like never before or afterward for Marx, generating new discoveries in his oeuvre (detailed in the next chapter).

More informed about Marx's views on the race question, coauthor Kyle Edwards and I added an essay to the 2024 book—one of two appendices—that addressed some of Marx's critics on that contentious matter.The republication of *Black Marxism* in 2000 gave unprecedented prominence to Robinson's claims. Four of the five critics rely on Robinson's book for authority, including his claims about how Du Bois regarded Marx. The fifth, a "friendly" critic, reveals how even a sympathetic Marx voice could err on the fraught issue. My essay, therefore, confronts Robinson anew by interrogating those who employ *Black Marxism* for wisdom about the real Marx.

But my 2024 essay challenges Robinson directly. In chapter 9 in *Black Marxism*, "Historiography and the Black Radical Tradition," Robinson makes a number of charges about "Marxism," "Bolshevism," "Communism" in the United States in relation to "the Negro Question," and the role of the "less gifted epigoni." The essay, more informed about the real Marx project, including some of his "epigoni" like Trotsky and Du Bois as well, than the 1985 review, provides an alternative narrative to Robinson's key claim about the Marxists not getting it right when it came to "Black Nationalism." By no means sufficient in debunking that charge, the essay constitutes the beginning of such a refutation.

Except for spelling corrections or a stylistic improvement here and there, this copy is faithful to the original. The occasional "we," "our," and "book" refer to co-author Kyle Edwards and I and our Marx-Douglass book in which the essay first appeared.

"Marx and Engels on the Race Question: A Response to the Critics"

(From Nimtz and Edwards, *The Communist and Revolutionary Liberal in the Second American Revolution: Comparing Karl Marx and Frederick Douglass in Real-Time* (Leiden, The Netherlands: Brill, 2024; republished as a paperback by Haymarket Press in 2025.)

In the Introduction to her 2016 collection, *The Civil War in the*

United States: Karl Marx & Friedrich Engels, Angela Zimmerman raises what she calls "shortcomings" in Marx and Engels with regard to race, racism, and white supremacy, limiting, she claims, "their ability to analyze the Civil War." Because Zimmerman has performed an invaluable service for Marxist scholarship in republishing the Richard Enmale 1937 collection of the Marx and Engels writings on the war, and translating and adding to the collection the all-so-important Weydemeyer articles, her criticisms have to be taken seriously.[3] An entire book or two could be devoted to other, less friendly, critics of Marx and Engels on the topic. This appendix addresses only those whose criticisms are relevant to this book's project, beginning with Zimmerman.[4]

Marx and Engels's usage of the "n-word," an issue addressed in our Introduction, is the "shortcoming" Zimmerman begins with. But they "used this term," to repeat, "ironically . . . to highlight a racism that they criticized rather than endorsed. Marx and Engels opposed racism at every turn, and the communist movements that they inspired have remained some of the most powerful and consistent anti-racist and anti-imperialist forces in the world, including the United States." We are largely in agreement with Zimmerman, given what I wrote on the matter in 2003, which we reproduced in the Introduction. Again, "Marx began to use 'nigger' during the Civil War as he was familiarizing himself with the U.S. reality. In published writings he always employed quotation marks; in letters often without. Only once, it seems, did he use it in a derogatory sense" (more about this later).[5]

The next "shortcoming" Zimmerman raises has to do with a comment Marx made to Engels in an 1853 letter. "When Marx remarked, in 1853, that US blacks who were born into slavery were not 'freshly imported barbarians' from Africa but rather 'a native product, more or less Yankeefied, English speaking, etc., and hence capable of being emancipated' (document 104 [in the

2016 Zimmerman collection]), he did not only denigrate African cultures; he also blinded himself to the many African and African American political traditions that contributed to the defeat of slavery in the Americas."[6]

From Zimmerman, that's a serious charge because it suggests that Marx would have been unprepared and therefore have missed any "African and African American" initiatives in the leadup to and during the Civil War; a real shortcoming for the revolutionary that Marx purported to be. Is that true?

But first, what did Marx actually say to Engels? Zimmerman's point refers to what Marx thought about the just-published *The Slave Trade, Domestic and Foreign* by America's leading economist Henry Carey, a fan of Marx . . . to whom he had gifted a copy.

> The only thing of definite interest in the book is the comparison between Negro slavery as formerly practiced by the English in Jamaica and elsewhere, and Negro slavery in the United States. He demonstrates how the main STOCK of Negroes in Jamaica always consisted of freshly imported BARBARIANS, since their treatment by the English meant not only that the Negro population was not maintained, but also that two-thirds of the yearly imports always went to waste, whereas the present generation of Negroes in America is a native product, more or less Yankeefied, English speaking, etc., and hence *capable of being emancipated*.[7]

"Barbarians" seems to have bothered Zimmerman. But Marx was quoting what was in the original as the editors of the *Marx-Engels Collected Works* customarily indicate with the small capitalization. "In the islands," Carey wrote, "the slave was generally a barbarian, speaking an unknown tongue . . . [whereas] here [the United States], he was generally a being born on the soil, speaking the same language with his owner." Further on, according to Carey: "In the islands, everything looked toward the permanency of slavery. Here, everything looked toward the gradual and gentle civilization and emancipation of the negro throughout the world."[8]

Given what Carey wrote, we read Marx's "capable of being emancipated" to mean no more than that the prospects for the enslaved would be improved by those of them who had mastered English. Douglass, it seems to us, epitomized Marx's point; his usage of English to advance the cause for abolition was exemplary. As David Blight puts it, "Douglass was a man of words; spoken and written language was the only major weapon of protest, persuasion, or power that he ever possessed."[9] Manisha Sinha emphasizes that Douglass's first autobiography, his narrative, made "the slave's indictment of slavery the most effective weapon in the abolitionist arsenal and for popularizing the genre."[10] That Douglass spoke and wrote English so powerfully certainly gives credence to the claim that American slaves were capable of being emancipated.

Why what Marx underscored translates, as Zimmerman charges, into the denigration of "African cultures" or being "blinded . . . to the many African and African American political traditions that contributed to the defeat of slavery in the Americas" is not clear. By bringing Douglass into the picture, as our book does, that lack of clarity is exposed—what comparisons can reveal as Marx pointed out to Engels.

Once the war began, Zimmerman finds problematic Marx's initial comment about Union prospects in May 1861. Her chief complaint about Marx and Engels: "When he called 'slave revolution' the 'last card up its [Union] sleeve,' he attributes agency to the white Northern leadership who might play this card rather than to enslaved black workers themselves." The bookend to that comment for Zimmerman is Marx's oft-quoted sentence in his

1867 magnum opus: "When Marx wrote in *Capital* that 'Labor cannot emancipate itself in the white skin where in the black it is branded,' he connected the struggles of white and black workers, but also suggested that they were separate." The crux of Marx and Engels's problem, according to Zimmerman, is that they "missed . . . the largest worker rebellion of all at the heart of the Union victory and the Civil War: the determination of great numbers of the four million enslaved black workers to withdraw their labor from their erstwhile masters, to transform the war for the Union into a war against slavery, and to throw their collective intelligence, capacity for labor, and armed might behind the Union."[11] Quite a claim and indictment.

Despite Zimmerman's criticisms, she ends on a positive note. If Marx and Engels didn't fully appreciate the enslaved as a Black proletariat, their comrades in the War—Weydemeyer in particular, who "worked with, and fought alongside" them—did. "All this suggests" the lesson "that the fight against racism is not a matter of white people perfecting their own 'un-racist' ideas but rather develops through interracial political solidarity." We wholeheartedly agree, wisdom that today's virtue-signalling social justice warriors could surely benefit from.[12]

But was it true that "the largest worker rebellion," that is, the withdrawal by the enslaved of "their labor from their erstwhile masters," brought down the slavocracy and that Marx and Engels failed to recognize that fact? These are two interrelated but separate claims. While historian James Oakes gives credence to the first one, he and other Civil War historians soberly point out that when Lee surrendered to Grant at Appomattox in April 1865, at least 80 percent of the enslaved were still in bondage.[13] Freedom for them, as had been true from the beginning of the war, depended on the battlefield progress of Union troops as in Galveston, Texas, on June 19, 1865—the now celebrated Juneteenth. Resistance, to employ Lenin's point four decades later in the context of Russia's 1905 Revolution, could take either an active or a passive form; preferable was the former.[14] While the quotidian resistance of their chattel slaves still bounded to the plantation no doubt corroded the slave oligarchy's infrastructure and undermined eventual victory for them, only an organized and disciplined Union Army, finally welcoming Blacks and former slaves alongside European immigrants and native-born white toilers, could actually bring them to heel—what Appomattox registered.

As for Zimmerman's charge that Marx and Engels were derelict in not crediting Black toilers with agency and underappreciating their role in the defeat of the Confederacy, let's bring Douglass into the conversation—something that our comparison can uniquely do. Real-time analysis requires examining events as they actually unfold.

The actual record reveals that Marx, if anything, overestimated the "agency" of the enslaved, beginning with the John Brown raid. Although Engels later said that Brown "did more than anyone else in the abolition of slavery,"[15] a *white* abolitionist, in other words—the advantages of hindsight no doubt—in real-time he and his partner thought the raid's significance was the spark it lit for a slave rebellion. For a brief moment that looked like a real possibility, but it soon proved not to be the case. Douglass serves as the best real-time voice for assessing Zimmerman's suggestion that Blacks were in a position to set the agenda for emancipation. As Marx might have said, they could indeed exercise free will but not "under self-selected circumstances," that is, of their own choosing.

From the very beginning, Douglass made that clear. In his first comment about how to respond to the slave oligarchy's attack on Fort Sumter in April 1861, he wrote: "Let the slaves and free colored people be called into service and formed into a liberating army." Douglass's "be called" speaks to the reality in that moment: the Union government was calling the shots. Nine months later, he reported that he had "been often asked since the war began why I am not in the South battling for freedom." The reason, he said, with apparent frustration, was that the government "does not yet rank me or [nota bene] my race with men."[16] Douglass's agency for participating in the war, in other words, was limited by decisions and actions of the Lincoln administration. Two years later, after Lincoln had just issued the final Emancipation Proclamation, Douglass wrote on the front page of his *Monthly*, "The colored men of the North have remained silent . . . now waiting to be honorably invited forward. . . . Let the government say the word."[17]

What about the enslaved in the Confederacy? Did they have more agency, as Zimmerman suggests? And were Marx and Engels derelict for not appreciating that fact? Our excavation of their corpus, to briefly recapitulate, reveals three antebellum Marx utterances of possible relevance. First, Marx's first reference to slaves in 1842 and his implicit assumption that they were capable of being educated in ways that their slave masters feared and thus the need to censor what they might read.[18] Exhibit A, Douglass. Second, in 1847, Marx's lecture in which he disputed the assumption that being "a Negro" was equivalent to being "a slave." To know someone's social status did not necessarily say anything about who they actually were and [what they were] capable of doing—a lecture to be revisited.[19] And third, about 1857, a slave, like a proletarian, was also capable of being "conscious" about what it meant to be free. Think Douglass.[20] Marx, in other words, should, in theory, have been primed to quickly recognize Black agency once the slavocracy fired on Fort Sumter in April 1861.

When we get to the Civil War, the consensus of the literature, again, is that the proximity of Union troops was determinant. Douglass recognized that fact in his coverage of the escape, weeks into the war, of the three slaves to the Union's Fortress Monroe in Virginia. The problem Douglass considered paramount in the early months of the war was Confederate use of slave labor to shore up its prospects. Not until the issuance of the preliminary Emancipation Proclamation at the end of September 1862 could Douglass happily report for the first time on large numbers of former slaves fleeing to Union lines. But again, flight depended on the progress of Union troops and, in the end, on Lee's surrender to Grant in April 1865.

Only when Lincoln made it official in early 1863 that Black men would be welcomed into the Union Army did onetime slaves effectively ensure Union victory. What Zimmerman fails to grasp, or perhaps agree with—a fundamental premise of Marx's and Engels's perspective—is that to be enslaved was to be unfree to exercise self-determination in a way that a worker could. Unlike a slave, a worker—Marxism 101—could choose their exploiter and all that implied, such as being able to sign up for the Union Army when the opportunity presented itself. In the real world of the Civil War, the enslaved had to wait for the arrival of that army—which included, after mid-1863, former bondsmen—to exercise choice. If agency for Zimmerman refers to the enslaved deciding to flee to Union lines when their forces got close enough, then we have no quarrel with her.[21] And if "the largest worker rebellion" means for Zimmerman an alliance of small white farmers, white and recently created Black workers that brought down the Slave Power, we are in complete accord with her.[22] Nothing we know of in Marx and Engels's commentary would be in disagreement. Unlike Zimmerman, evidently, we read her astute point that "their comrades," like Joseph Weydemeyer, "who served in the Union Army . . . worked with, and fought alongside, formerly enslaved African Americans . . . gained a better understanding of the importance of black workers in the conflict" to be a compliment to the Marx party, the advantages of organized collective work—the ersatz party that Douglass lacked. Until the end, Weydemeyer considered that he was carrying out a line that his two comrades in England would have agreed with. If Zimmerman thinks otherwise, she should say so.

A telling coda. Two decades later, Marx again overestimated Black agency when he mistakenly thought that new Republican president Rutherford B. Hayes's withdrawal of federal troops from the South in 1877 would spark a militant Black response. Douglass, like many other leading middle-class Blacks now in bed with the Republican Party, knew better—circumstances not of Marx's choosing.[23]

One last point about Zimmerman's criticisms, a bit ironic in our opinion. W. E. B. Du Bois's masterful *Black Reconstruction,* she correctly notes, stands on the shoulders of Marx and Engels's Civil War writings. His notion of the "general strike," the means by which "these black workers transformed the war between the Union and the Confederacy into a revolution against slavery," in fact inspired her claim about "the largest worker rebellion of all at the heart of the Union victory." Marx and Engels's writings, in other words, and despite Zimmerman's charge about their myopia regarding Black toilers, inexplicably inspired subsequent analysts to see Black agency, including, by way of Du Bois, Zimmerman herself. That apparent contradiction explains, perhaps, why we can regard Zimmerman as a friendly critic of "Marx and Engels on Race."

We can't say the same when it comes to Wulf Hund, in fact a disingenuous critic in our opinion. We begin with him in his own words, from the abstract to his 2021 article, "Marx and Haiti: Note on a Blank Space."[24] Marx, according to Hund, "ignored the history of the revolution in Haiti"

> because of his deficient analysis of contemporary racism. This is made clear in relation to 1) his acceptance of the biological meaning of race, 2) his involvement in two main racisms of his time, antisemitism and colonial racism, and 3) his differentiation and (de)gradation of historical subjects. The consequences were dramatic, not because of Marx's involvement in the racist zeitgeist, but insofar as his learning process with regard to the relevance of anticolonial movements and his awareness of negative societalization, as well as its significance, were not reflected in a theory of racism. This was to prove a debacle for subsequent attempts at a Marxist analysis of racism and has had effects that are still evident today.[25]

The focus here is only on Hund's claims about Marx as they relate to this book. Let's begin with what we think is obvious. If Hund is to be believed, Marx should have been missing in action in responding to modernity's first major step in eradicating the "racist zeitgeist," the abolition of chattel slavery in the United States. Because he lacked "a theory of racism," Marx—this is implicit in Hund's rendering of him—would have been incapable of being on the right side in that history-defining moment. Hund's critique is only implied, I argue, because he knows exactly how Marx responded to the slave oligarchy's attack on Fort Sumter in April 1861. Hund read, in fact, what I wrote in 2003 about that response, in many ways a preview of this book. Rather than directly contest Marx's own antiracist credentials—revealed in action and not in theory—Hund, therefore, faults Marx for the sins of those who later claimed to speak in his name on the topic of race, an issue to be revisited.

Hund's first charge, Marx's alleged "acceptance of the biological meaning of race," refers to the aforementioned passage in his 1847 "Wage Labor and Capital" lecture that begins with "What is a Negro?" Here's the entire text:

> What is a Negro slave? A man of the black race. The one explanation is as good as the other. A Negro is a Negro. He only becomes a *slave* in certain relations. A cotton-spinning jenny is a machine for spinning cotton. It becomes *capital* only in certain relations. Torn from these relations it is no more capital than *gold* in itself is *money* or sugar the *price* of sugar.[26]

Here is what I wrote in 2003 about the passage:

> Marx was, as it might be called in some academic settings today, deconstructing the concept of "Negro." By the mid-nineteenth century, in Western Europe at least, Black identity had become increasingly synonymous with servitude. This was especially true in the United States where—especially in slave states—with each succeeding decade of the nineteenth century the laws and courts made the condition of "free Blacks" increasingly impossible. Marx, therefore challenged the racist conclusions about Blacks that derived from their oppression and exploitation.[27]

For Hund, on the other hand, Marx's response to his opening question, "A man of the Black race," is irrefutable proof that Marx subscribed to a "biological meaning of race." And for me to have written, Hund charges, that Marx was "deconstructing the concept of 'Negro'" was to be "uncritical and disguises the problem contained in Marx's statement. . . . Marx recognizes only one dimension of the racism at issue; slavery is not natural. But he does not realize the other racist dimension of his deliberation; for him, race theory is valid and being a 'Negro' is a natural quality, not a social relation."[28] But is that true?

Hund certainly knows that Marx, like so many others of that era, including Frederick Douglass, employed "race" most often to refer to what today is usually called ethnicity and/or nationality.

For example, their frequent references to the English, the German, the Russian, the Irish, etc. "races." At the same time, Douglass would certainly have agreed with Marx calling him "a man of the Black race" as in the aforementioned self-described "of my race."[29] Would Hund then accuse Douglass, like Marx, of "involvement in the racist zeitgeist" of that era? What conclusions, if so, are to be drawn from such a usage? Given its then different meanings, does Hund know for sure what Marx meant by "race" in that passage, before social Darwinism and its biological connotations of race had become *de rigueur* in intellectual circles? Hund, at least, owes it to his readers to inform them about the then various usages of the term.

If Hund is accusing Marx of not knowing what science later revealed, that race is an invention, a social construction without any kind of biological justification, then he's right and why he can appear to be smarter than not only Marx and Douglass but virtually anyone else from that era to at least the middle of the twentieth century regarding race. More meaningful is the "so what" question when it comes to Marx, the quintessential revolutionary. Did his understanding of "race" impede or advance his revolutionary project?

Once again, the overthrow of precapitalist modes of production like chattel slavery for Marx was indispensable for the full development of capitalist relations of production. With the latter came the proletariat, the first oppressed layer in the history of class society that had a class interest in the abolishment of private property, the material basis of social inequality and hence racial inequality. Whatever his understanding of "race," Marx and his comrades in the United States single-mindedly did all they could to put an end to America's peculiar institution, the most effective antiracist work of the nineteenth century. Compared to any contemporaries, including Douglass, Marx was exemplary.

We suspect that Hund, as academics like him all too often do, reads Marx in his own image, primarily a theory-maker and not as a revolutionary activist. "Ideas," the young Marx concluded in 1844, "cannot carry out anything at all. In order to carry out ideas men are needed."[30] Three years later, Engels tried to explain to an opponent what he and his partner stood for:

> Communism is not a doctrine but a movement, it proceeds not from principles but from facts. . . . Communism, insofar as it is a theory, is the theoretical expression of the position of the proletariat in this struggle ["between proletariat and bourgeoisie"] and the theoretical summation of the conditions for the liberation of the proletariat.[31]

We suspect, also, that they fault Marx for not having a "theory of race," or of nationalism, or perhaps gender, because they fundamentally disagree with his communism and its proletariat-centric explanation for ending social inequality—and are disingenuous in not being forthright in saying so.[32] We take our lead from Engels, the person who knew him best. "'Marx was," as Engels put it at his partner's funeral in 1883, "before all else a revolutionist."[33] For the Civil War, the longest revolutionary moment that Marx ever lived through, the primary task was to do all he could to ensure the military defeat of the slave oligarchy and, thus, the birth of a hereditary proletariat throughout the United States for the first time. Marx assumed from the beginning that the North would be victorious because, if needed, Lincoln had a "last card up his sleeve . . . a slave rebellion." But an unknown factor that could delay or even prevent that victory would be the response of "poor whites" in the South to the oligarchy's pro-slavery war.

Long before the war began, Marx knew about the ideas that rationalized racial slavery. *Marie, or Slavery in America,* the 1835 novel about an ill-fated interracial romance by Tocqueville's travel companion, Gustave de Beaumont, was probably his first detailed introduction to the topic. Subsequent reading helped to explain the prevailing mid-nineteenth-century belief in much of the trans-Atlantic world that to be "a Negro slave" was to be "a man of the black race"—exactly what he contested in his 1847 "Wage Labor and Capital" lecture. Never for a moment did Marx doubt that America's peculiar institution was a quintessentially class institution, that is, one in which one layer of society lived off the uncompensated labor of another. That the exploited came exclusively in Black skin and that the exploiters, beginning with the three hundred thousand slave owners, employed racial claims to sustain and defend the practice didn't make it any less a class institution. The slave oligarchy's foundational documents like Hammond's 1858 "mudsill speech" and Confederate vice president Alexander Stephens's December 1860 speech, both with which Marx was familiar, made that fact all so clear. No "theory of race," in other words, was needed to explain why the slave oligarchs actively played the race card—it was in their class interests to do so, or, as Douglass often put it, it was due to greed.

But, again, what about "poor whites," the "white trash" as the oligarchs contemptuously called them? Why did they embrace the slave oligarchy's racial agenda? Why would it have been, that is, in their class interest to do so? Our close reading of Marx reveals an explanation he offered, one either underappreciated or unknown until now. For Marx, it was, again, "the bait" or "the lure" of upward mobility for white plebeians in the South that explained their embrace of the slave oligarchs' expansionist agenda, the possibility that they too could one day become slave owners. And embracing that agenda entailed the embrace of its racist ideology. Douglass had, as a slave, personally experienced the anti-Black "prejudices" of "poor whites," specifically, white co-workers on the docks in Baltimore, many of Irish origin. He didn't think, however, that those ideas were inherent, but learned behaviors, probably a later realization after his first visit to Ireland in 1845 when he discovered that anti-Black attitudes were nonexistent there. Marx likely knew the same owing to his familiarity with the German immigrant experience to America. But Marx offered a material reason for the embrace of the racist ideas. Douglass's explanation came closer, it seems to us, to what W. E. B. Du Bois would call in *Black Reconstruction* "a sort of public and psychological wage" used by the Jim Crow ruling class to compensate the white working class, "because they were white."[34] But behind the "psychological wage" for Marx—if that's the appropriate label—was, again, the enticement of the material perks that came with "whiteness."

Whether Marx's explanation constitutes "a theory of racism" for Hund or other similar critics is for them to decide. For Marx the revolutionary, the issue of Southern white plebeians possibly breaking with the slavocracy was enormously important in that moment. His detailed attention to the secession votes in the slave-owning states was driven by that question. That secession, he concluded, was largely an elite affair without the consent of "poor whites" was instructive for Marx. Trying, in other words, to understand what motivated the latter was an elementary communist obligation: Southern prospects depended on the recruitment of white plebeians. As it turned out, the increasing alienation of "poor whites" from the "rich man's war" proved to be consequential in the Confederacy's defeat—maybe as important as the passive resistance of the enslaved.[35]

If Marx didn't have "a theory of race," he certainly had a theory about social inequality: it rested on private property. Only the proletariat, unlike a slave, for example, had a class interest, he held, in ending private property, the prerequisite for its own emancipation. Getting rid of all obstacles, therefore, to making the proletariat the ruling class, such as feudalism and chattel slavery, was the number one task of communists. That's the basic assumption, the theory, that informed Marx's practice and that of his comrades in the United States and elsewhere, the Marx party, both prior to and after Fort Sumter.

A theory of race has to begin with the fact that "race," like nationality, is a moving target—an invention or social construct, as it is sometimes called today. More grounded in material reality is the inherently exploitative reality of class relations once class society came into existence about ten thousand years ago.[36] Its most recent edition, capitalism, birthed a new exploited class, the proletariat, who could only survive by selling its labor to owners of private property and, hence, again, could only liberate itself by ending private property. If that claim makes Marx a class fundamentalist, as some might charge, we're confident that he would have pleaded guilty, especially if the alternative was some kind of race, national, or maybe gender fundamentalism, to name only a few current candidates. Even when it came to his magnum opus *Capital,* Marx in 1877, a decade after its publication, advised caution about how to read his theory. Regarding his chapter on "Primitive Accumulation," he faulted a critic for wanting "to metamorphose my historical sketch of the genesis of capitalism in Western Europe into a historical-philosophical theory of general development, imposed by fate on all peoples, whatever the historical circumstances in which they are placed."[37] For the same reason, it is hard to imagine Marx wanting to have some kind of "theory about race" that could be applicable to different realities in both place and time. That ruling elites, be they slave oligarchs or capitalists, employed ideas to divide the toilers is probably the most that Marx might have ventured about the theory of race, as in his 1869–1870 comments about the similarities between anti-Irish and anti-Black attitudes among, respectively, English and American white workers—an issue to be revisited. As to why the latter two groups of workers bought into such ideas, Marx, we suspect, would have been satisfied with his lure-of-upward-mobility explanation.

Before turning to Hund's claim that Marx's lack of a "theory of racism" proved to be "a debacle for subsequent attempts at a Marxist analysis of racism and has bad effects that are still evident today," we briefly address some of his other criticisms of Marx.

To Hund's charge that Marx's failure to say anything in detail about the Haitian Revolution registered his buy-in to anti-Black attitudes then in vogue, our response, again, is that it is Hund who is derelict—for not acknowledging Marx's revolutionary response to the nineteenth-century's decisive moment in the struggle against racism. Whatever was lacking in Marx's oeuvre on Haiti clearly was not to his disadvantage in doing the right thing when the slave oligarchy attacked Fort Sumter—probably the reason for Hund's deafening silence about Marx's practice during the Civil War. It would be easy to dismiss Hund's complaint for that reason alone, but what he raises about the Haitian Revolution offers an opportunity to gain a better appreciation of Marx's communist project on the eve of the Civil War.

There was a very consequential actor in the leadup to the war who had studied the Haitian Revolution in detail. Probably no one in the United States knew as much about modern history's first successful slave revolt as John Brown did. The autodidact read everything he could about the revolution as preparation for his project.[38] But did it make Brown more effective, as Hund's complaint about Marx might suggest? That would be a dubious claim. For Marx and Engels, again, the significance of Brown's failed attack was the likelihood that it sparked a slave uprising, a development, if Hund is to be believed, about which Marx would have been dismissive. The "most momentous thing happening in the world today," Marx told Engels at the beginning of 1860, "is the slave movement—on the one hand in America, started by the death of Brown, and in Russia, on the other."[39] Brown, we argue, would have been better off reading the *Communist Manifesto*. But, as in the case of the economist Henry Carey and Douglass, the absence of a hereditary proletariat in the United States would have likely made the document incomprehensible to Brown. Douglass no doubt knew about Brown's expertise on the Haitian Revolution, but that wasn't enough to convince him to join his attack on the armory at Harpers Ferry. What might have made sense for Haiti in 1794 did not for America in 1859.

Hund also takes Marx to task for alleged antisemitism; his first evidence, Marx's 1843–1844 articles, "The Jewish Question." We referenced these in the first chapter of this book [see introduction] because of what they taught about Marx's trajectory toward communist conclusions, specifically the lessons from America about the buying and selling of everything.[40] For Hund, the articles betray Marx's subscription to *en vogue* anti-Jewish stereotypes. We disagree and still find persuasive Hal Draper's detailed retort to that long-made accusation.[41] Hund, in search of evidence for his anti-Marx thesis, misses the significance of the articles. If the United States was the best that liberal democracy had to offer, then clearly something else was required to end its social inequalities, including that of chattel slavery, perpetuated and deepened by its market mania, in order to realize "true democracy," or "human emancipation." That conclusion helps to explain why Marx could be ready to aid and abet the abolition of America's peculiar institution when the opportunity presented itself.

More damaging, in Hund's opinion, is Marx's characterization of Ferdinand Lassalle in a letter to Engels in 1862: "The Jewish

NIGGER Lassalle . . . is descended from the negroes who accompanied Moses' flight from Egypt (unless his mother or paternal grandmother interbred with a NIGGER. . . . The fellow's importunity is also niggerlike."[42] This is the comment I was referring to when I wrote in 2003 about Marx's usage of the *n*-word: "Only once, it seems, did he use it in a derogatory sense, in a diatribe against Ferdinand Lassalle." I added that any of his and Engels's comments "in personal correspondence that were unambiguously racist, sexist or antisemitic must be seen in context in relation to their entire corpus of writings and actions."[43] To be considered alongside that disparagement of Lassalle is what Marx told his wife, Jenny, upon learning that Lassalle was mortally wounded two years later, the result of a duel about an embarrassing love affair: "We were genuinely dismayed by the news since, whatever one may say L[assalle] is too good to go under in this way."[44] The Marx-Lassalle relationship was obviously complicated and can't be reduced to a one-off comment that Marx made in rage about someone he felt to be "too good" to meet an ignominious end.[45] Nor is it certain, contrary to Hund, what meaning Marx assigned to "nigger," "negro," or "niggerlike." To repeat what I wrote in 2003: "For what it's worth, Marx was fondly known by close friends and family as 'Moor' owing to his dark features and had a son-in-law, Paul Lafargue, a mulatto, who was also fondly called in family circles, 'African,' 'Negro' and 'Negrillo.'" This suggests that one should be cautious and not rush to judgment based on the vapid criteria of "political correctness." I stand by that assessment. The issue of antisemitism merits a revisit.

Marx's above-mentioned comments in the April 1870 letter about the similarities between anti-Black and anti-Irish attitudes by respectively "poor whites" and "English workers" draws Hund's final critique of Marx. Here's the actual passage that is the target of Hund's ire:

> The ordinary English worker hates the Irish worker as a competitor who forces down the STANDARD OF LIFE. In relation to the Irish worker, he feels himself to be a member of the *ruling nation* and, therefore, makes himself a tool of his aristocrats and capitalists *against Ireland*, thus strengthening their domination *over himself*. He harbours religious, social and national prejudices against him. His attitude towards him is roughly that of the POOR WHITES to the NIGGERS in the former slave states of the American Union.[46]

Hund—whose transcription of the passage doesn't include the small capitalization that indicates terms in the original English—criticizes the remark by saying that it's an inappropriate comparison, apples and oranges, mixing race and class categories, and in so doing Marx deprecated the Irish by comparing them to "the niggers." But with his focus on theory-making, Hund missed or, perhaps, ignored the real story—Marx's correction of his prior position on the Irish struggle. Contrary to Hund's charge, he now elevated "the Irish question." Five months before the April 1870 letter, with the passage that Hund inadequately quotes, Marx explained to Engels his change of opinion:

> For a long time I believed it would be possible to overthrow the Irish regime by ENGLISH WORKING CLASS ASCENDANCY. I always took this viewpoint in the *New-York Tribune*. Deeper study has now convinced me of the opposite. The English WORKING CLASS will *never accomplish anything* BEFORE IT HAS GOT RID OF IRELAND. The lever must be applied in Ireland. This is why the Irish QUESTION is so important for the social movement in general.[47]

As the effective head of the International Workingmen's Association (IWMA), Marx's task, he told Engels, was to convince the English labor leaders on the General Council of the IWMA of his new position—"the thing now," to another correspondent, "is to drum this conviction into the English working class"—a goal that proved elusive owing largely to the attitudes of the labor aristocracy from which virtually all of those leaders originated.[48]

The background to this change of position was the new upsurge in the Irish struggle for self-determination and the support it was winning in England itself. A mass demonstration for amnesty for Irish political prisoners in London on October 24, 1869, that his youngest daughter Eleanor insisted her parents attend, seems to have made the difference. She had recently returned from an extended visit with Engels and his Irish nationalist wife, Lizzie Burns, in Manchester and came back to London an ardent defender of the Irish struggle. Thus, it was the agency of the Irish struggle itself that convinced Marx to change his position, the communist obligation to learn from the real movement, as Engels once explained in 1847.

The significance of Marx's correction can't be overstated; and about which there is not even a hint of it in Hund's narrative. One of only three corrections in my reading of his and Engels's corpus—the other two being the self-criticism of the 1850 Address about how communists should participate in elections and the new 1872 preface to the *Communist Manifesto*, owing to what the Paris Commune had taught about the state—it would have enormous importance for his followers in the twentieth century.[49] Hund, on the other hand, uses the passage from the April 1870 letter and the one from *Capital* about "Labour in white skin" to accuse Marx of not giving agency to Blacks, similar to Zimmerman's charge that I've already addressed.

Time now to turn to what happened to Marx's project with regard to the race question after his death. Did Marx and Engels bequeath their followers enough kernels of wisdom with which to be creative when the real movement of history demanded that they be so—as communists, and not as academic theory-makers? Or did the project lead, as Hund claims, to a "debacle" for his followers, owing to his failure not to have bequeathed them a "theory of racism"—Hund's main charge? Again, and not to beat a dead horse, Marx, according to Hund's logic, should have flunked the most important test of his lifetime on the race question because he lacked a "theory of racism." No wonder, then, the deafening silence in his account of Marx's practice during the U.S. Civil War. To have recognized in any sustained way what Marx did would render null and void his claim, beginning with Marx himself. Only at the end does Hund actually address his primary argument about the lacuna in Marx's oeuvre:

> This had lasting impacts on the handling of racism within the wing of the labor movement that was based on Marxist ideas and not least on the Marxist theory itself. Even if we assume the existence of various Marxisms, their exponents either viewed racism as a subordinate problem or did not bring the debate on the relationship between class and race to a consensual conclusion; in addition, they did not bring the analysis of two of the main racisms of modernity, antisemitism and colonial racism, to a common denominator.[50]

But for such a sweeping claim—probably inspired by Robinson's *Black Marxism*—Hund ends with at best five hundred words for evidence. Titling his critique a "note" doesn't absolve Hund from providing something more substantive. What does the actual record reveal about the "lasting impacts"?

Marx didn't live long enough to witness the bloody overthrow of Reconstruction. Even when Engels died in 1895, the United

States Supreme Court had yet to make the defeat official with its infamous *Plessy v. Ferguson* decision the following year. The lack-of-theory complaint by Hund and others, we suspect, is about the racist counterrevolution, an outcome that the critics seem to think that Marx and Engels should have anticipated. But even Douglass, more intimately familiar with what was underway, as we document, had difficulty explaining that outcome.

The complaint, in our view, is the wisdom of hindsight. Real-time analysis, rather, is the best test of theory and perspective. Not for naught did Du Bois, in his 1933 article in the NAACP's *Crisis* magazine, "Karl Marx and the Negro," end on a note of regret. "It was a great loss to American Negroes that the great mind of Marx and his extraordinary insight into industrial conditions could not have been brought to bear at first hand upon the history of the American Negro between 1876 and the World War."[51] Explaining the overthrow of Reconstruction, in other words, would have surely benefited, Du Bois believed, from Marx's real-time examination.

Du Bois sought to make up for Marx's missing analysis with one of his own, his 1935 magisterial *Black Reconstruction,* inspired by many of Marx's insights. Because of the volume's renown, Hund is forced to admit, contrary to his argument, that students of Marx, like Du Bois, could theorize on race even though their mentor hadn't left them anything, apparently, upon which to do so. Hund, unsurprisingly, can't resist finding something deficient in Du Bois's tome: "He never expanded these deliberations [based on his reading of Marx] towards a general theory of racism (including antisemitism and other forms of racist exclusion not based on color racism)."[52] Frantz Fanon, who also looked to Marx, is guilty of the same failing because he "never expanded on both deliberations [the similarities between anti-Black and anti-Jewish prejudices] towards a general theory of racism."[53]

Nothing less than a unified field theory of race for all places and time can satisfy Hund. His protests to the contrary, Hund comes close to naturalizing—in fact arguably naturalizes—something called "race," about which there can be "a general theory."

Another student of Marx also challenges Hund's claim that his racial "blind spot" incapacitated them for saying anything meaningful not only about the race/class nexus but also the Haitian Revolution. Marxist historian C. L. R. James is a particularly inconvenient figure for Hund's thesis. His still influential 1938 analysis of the Revolution, *The Black Jacobins: Toussaint L'Ouverture and the San Domingo Revolution*, was inspired by rather than handicapped by Marx's analysis, especially, his *Eighteenth Brumaire* and its opening thesis: "Men make their own history, but they do not make it as they please; they do not make it under self-selected circumstances, but under circumstances existing already, given and transmitted from the past."[54] Until the end of his life James considered himself to be a Marxist revolutionary. For that reason, most likely, Hund could not bring himself to include James's book in the main text of his article but instead deeply buries it in a footnote.[55] And, as with his treatment of Du Bois's tome, Hund had to take a hit to James's *Black Jacobins*, his failure to "debate the 'blank space' . . . in the oeuvre of Marx (and Engels), nor . . . discuss their insufficient analysis of racism as the background of this peculiar silence."[56] Only a critique of Marx, as well as a "general theory of race," it seems, will satisfy Hund.

And then there is the heroic and also inconvenient example of Abram Leon. A devoted student of Marx, Leon titled his signature essay after his mentor's 1843–1844 *Zur Judenfrage* articles that Hund accuses of being antisemitic. Leon's 250-page manuscript, *The Jewish Question: A Marxist Interpretation*, completed two years before his death in the gas chambers at Auschwitz in 1944, does exactly what Hund claims a Marxist could not do.

Leon's findings, after a deep dive into ancient and medieval history, question Hund's argument that "a general theory of racism" must incorporate an explanation for both anti-Black and anti-Jewish prejudices. Owing to the almost caste-like role to which they were assigned for managing medieval finances, especially money-lending, Jews could uniquely serve capital, as it emerged as the dominant mode of production in the second half of the nineteenth century in Europe, as scapegoats for its sins. No other ethnic/racial group has ever been labeled a secret cabal that runs the world—conveniently deflecting attention away from the multiracial, multinational, and multigendered ruling class that actually does run the world today. Leon's conclusion that "there is no way to resolve the Jewish question independent of the world proletarian revolution" is as valid today as when he asserted it eight decades ago—a conclusion Hund would no doubt find unpalatable.[57] Some of us, nevertheless, find Leon's thesis to be a valuable teaching tool to help youth of all skin colors and creeds understand how a most ancient prejudice operates in today's capitalist world and why it is dangerous, its benign as well as its malignant manifestations.[58]

None of Marx's students was as consequential as, of course, Vladimir Ilich Lenin. Is he relevant to this discussion? Indeed, the above-mentioned comment about the significance of Marx's correction on the Irish struggle alluded to this. More informed about Marx and Engels's corpus than any of their students, Lenin corrected Rosa Luxemburg in his 1914 polemic, "The Right of Nations to Self-Determination." Contrary to her claim that independence for oppressed nationalities in empires such as Ireland would not be "practical," Lenin seized upon Marx's revision of his position on the Irish struggle in 1869. He quoted exactly the above-cited passage that Marx wrote to Engels on December 10 about his change of opinion, along with other exchanges between

Marx and Engels on the matter such as Marx's campaign inside the General Council of the IWMA: "I have done my best to bring about this demonstration of the English workers in favor of Fenianism [the ideology of Irish self-determination]." Then Lenin's distillation:

> At first Marx thought that Ireland would not be liberated by the national movement of the oppressed nation, but by the working-class movement of the oppressor nation.... Marx reconsidered his view and corrected it. "What a misfortune it is for a nation to have subjugated another." The English working class will never be free until Ireland is freed from the English yoke. Reaction in England is strengthened and fostered by the enslavement of Ireland (just as reaction in Russia is fostered by her enslavement of a number of nations!).... The policy of Marx and Engels on the Irish question serves as a splendid example of the attitude the proletariat of the oppressor nations should adopt towards national movements, an example which has lost none of its immense *practical* importance.[59]

Lenin's enthusiastic embrace of Marx's correction on the Irish question came to be one of the key programmatic differences that distinguished the Bolsheviks from other currents in the Socialist or Second International. The right of oppressed nations to self-determination became *de rigueur* for them not only for the Russian Revolution itself but for other anticolonial movements. Marx's correction would also have an echo inside the United States.

Until the Bolshevik Revolution, socialists in the United States tended to view the struggle for Black equality in the same manner that Marx had once viewed the Irish struggle in Great Britain, secondary to and/or dependent on the struggle of the proletariat, mainly, that is, the white working class. Just as Rosa Luxemburg evidently didn't know about Marx's revision, the same was true for American socialists—if they were attentive at all to Marx's project. And had they known Marx's change of opinion on the "Irish Question," they may not have made any connection with the "Negro Question." In the opinion of Socialist Party leader Eugene V. Debs, "We have nothing special to offer the Negro, and we cannot make separate appeals to all the races. The Socialist Party is the party of the whole working class, regardless of color—the whole working class of the whole world."[60] Though always appreciative of Debs's historical importance to the American theatre of the global class struggle, Lenin and the Bolsheviks had a different opinion.

To American radicals who were inspired by Russia's history-defining moment, the Bolshevik leaders sought to impress upon them what was "special" about the fight for equality for Black Americans. Lenin, in his "Theses on the National and Colonial Questions" for the Second Congress of the recently organized Communist International in 1920, was unequivocal: "All Communist parties must directly support the revolutionary movements among the nations that are dependent and do not have equal rights (for example Ireland, the Negroes in America, and so forth), and in the colonies. Without this last, especially important condition, the struggle against oppression of the dependent nations and colonies and recognition of their right to a separate state remain a dishonorable facade, such as we see in the parties of the Second International" with which the Socialist Party had been affiliated. Nota bene "Ireland" and "the Negroes in America"—echoes Marx's 1870 point about the similarities of Irish and Black American oppression that Hund dismisses as incomparable. For Lenin, in other words, the struggle for Black equality included the right to self-determination. Just as Marx had wanted "to drum . . . into the British working class" support for Irish self-determination, Lenin sought to do the same for those who claimed to be the communist vanguard of the American working class with regard to the Black struggle.

Lenin added to his directive. "The fight against . . . the most deeply rooted petty-bourgeois, nationalist prejudices (which are expressed in all possible forms, such as racism, national chauvinism, and anti-Semitism) must be given all the more priority as the question becomes more pressing of transforming the dictatorship of the proletariat from a national framework . . . into an international one."[61] The fight against scourges like racism was, in other words, indispensable for the international dictatorship of the proletariat, that is, the working class becoming the global ruling class, requiring, therefore, special attention. Also noteworthy is Lenin's inclusion of "anti-Semitism" along with the other hateful prejudices in his draft—supposedly absent, according to Hund, in Marxist discussions of the issue. Lenin obviously didn't feel that he was incapacitated in fighting against racism by not having been bequeathed, contrary to Hund, a "general theory of race" from Marx. But was he effective?

Given American radicalism's history of not lending special attention to the "Negro question," it should come as no surprise, as James P. Cannon, one of the founders of the American Communist Party later admitted, that "it took time for the Americans . . . to assimilate the new Leninist doctrine. But the Russians followed up year after year, piling up the arguments and increasing the pressure on the American communists until they finally learned and changed, and went to work in earnest. And the change in the attitude of the American communists, gradually effected in the twenties, was to exert a profound influence in far wider circles in the later years."[62] Cannon himself, to be seen shortly, tested the patience of the Russian comrades.

With Lenin incapacitated from March 1923 to his death ten months later, the stage was set for Stalin's ascent and the effective end to the best that the Russian Revolution had to offer the fledgling communist parties around the world, still inspired by the October Revolution. It fell to Leon Trotsky, Lenin's second in command of the Russian Revolution, to maintain continuity with his program. In forced exile, he counselled aspiring revolutionaries from all parts of the world, including the United States—the "profound influence . . . in the later years" that Cannon alluded to. Especially relevant for purposes here were his meetings with American comrades in 1933 and later in 1939.

For the first meeting, in Turkey, the key issue was whether his co-thinkers in the United States should promote, as the Stalinists there were doing, the slogan of self-determination for Black Americans or rather equal rights. He agreed with them that the slogan was opportunistic, having originated in Moscow and not from within Black America itself. Rather than criticizing the demand on the grounds that it led away from the class struggle, Trotsky countered that it was the racism of the white workers [cited in my 1985 review]— "ninety-nine point nine percent of the American workers are chauvinists; in relation to the Negroes they are hangmen as they are also toward the Chinese, etc."—that would be the blame, should significant separatist sentiment emerge among Blacks. His American co-thinkers, he continued, should be open to the idea of Blacks, especially the proletariat, making self-determination their demand because its logic had revolutionary implications. "It is very possible that the Negroes will proceed through self-determination to the proletarian dictatorship in a couple of giant strides, ahead of the great bloc of white workers. They will then be the vanguard. I am absolutely sure they will in any case fight better than the white workers. That, however, can happen only provided the communist party carries on an uncompromising struggle not against the

Negroes' supposed national prepossessions but against the colossal prejudices of white workers and make no concession to them whatever."[63] Like Marx and Lenin before him, Trotsky too sought "to drum this conviction," namely, support for self-determination for oppressed nationalities, into the vanguard of the American working class.

To the end, Trotsky campaigned for special attention to the "Negro Question" and defended the right of self-determination for African Americans. A year before his assassination in Mexico in 1940 at the hands of one of Stalin's many agents, Trotsky met with the aforementioned C. L. R. James, who was now a member of the American Socialist Workers Party, to discuss its perspectives for the struggle for Black equality there. He took issue with James's characterization of "self-determination" for African Americans as "reactionary . . . as a step backward so far as a socialist society is concerned."[64] For Blacks, Trotsky replied, to "fight for the possibility of realizing an independent state is a sign of great moral and political awakening. It would be a tremendous revolutionary step." In a letter to party leader James Cannon about the meeting, Trotsky wrote that what James presented at the meeting was a "very good statement," but

> I do not accept his categorical rejection of self-determination (an independent state) for the American Negro. As a party, we do not enter into the making of the decision, either one way or the other. We say to the Negroes, "You must decide whether or not you wish the separation. If you decide in the affirmative, we as a party will help you with all of our power to realize; and in this way the separation of states will assure the brotherhood of workers of both colors. This is what we want above all."[65]

More important for Trotsky about the meeting with James and

the two other party members in attendance was the opportunity it gave him to chide the party for not prioritizing the "Negro question," especially in the recruitment of Black workers:

> Many times I have proposed that every party member, especially intellectuals, who cannot win a worker-member to the party over a six-month period should be demoted to sympathiser, and the same in relation to winning Negro members. It is a question of the vitality of the party—of whether the party is transformed into a sect or is able to find its way to the most oppressed part of the working class.[66]

His patience wearing thin, he wrote to Cannon in the same April 10, 1939, letter that "the party . . . cannot postpone this extremely important question any longer." To the end, Trotsky sought "to drum" the urgency of the Black question into the vanguard of the workers movement in the United States. Not for naught did Cannon write two decades later:

> Everything new and progressive on the Negro question came from Moscow, after the revolution of 1917, and as a result of the revolution—not only for the American communists who responded directly, but for all others concerned with the question.[67]

The communist perspective on the right of oppressed nationalities for self-determination that began with Marx's correction on the Irish question and that Trotsky bequeathed to his followers in the United States paid major dividends for the Socialist Workers Party—what Cannon likely referred to regarding the "profound influence *in far wider circles* in the later years" that resulted from the drumming of the Bolsheviks. When the Black struggle took the form of Black nationalism in the 1960s, the party was theoretically equipped to advantageously respond to the opening. The communists with whom Malcolm X collaborated in the last year of his life . . . were precisely members of the Party. Even before he broke with the Nation of Islam and its Black separatist course, Socialist Workers Party (SWP) members were able to see the revolutionary implications of his discourse for a proletarian agenda and came to his defense against the race-baiting of the Stalinists and the violence-baiting of the government.

That Betty Shabazz, Malcolm X's widow, entrusted Pathfinder Press, the SWP's publishing arm, with keeping his speeches in print not only testifies to the fraternal relations that existed between him and the SWP at the time of his assassination but ensures that future fighters for racial equality can know what Malcolm X stood for in his own words. They'll be able to learn about his trajectory from a Black nationalist separatist to his political convergence with communists—a development that should have been impossible if Hund is to be believed. It is the same Pathfinder Press, by the way, that keeps in print not only the public declarations of Malcolm X in his final year, but also those of Trotsky and the record about how he convinced at least one Marxist current to prioritize the "Negro question," and the first book-length Marxist analysis of antisemitism, Leon's *The Jewish Question*. There is, therefore, at least one of the "various Marxisms," as Hund calls them, that promotes theoretical clarity for a set of complementary issues that Hund accuses Marxists of not addressing.

Another critique of Marx on the race question appeared the same year, 2021, as Hund's. Andrew Douglas's and Jared Loggins's *Prophet of Discontent* seeks to make a case for Martin Luther King Jr.'s revolutionary credentials. But to do so, the two scholars feel compelled to downgrade those of Marx on the grounds, according to the authorities they cite, that "when it comes to race, Marx missed the mark." Also, "Marx relegated 'as subsidiary the very things which should have been the center of his study.' "[68] Though at best a secondary theme in their essay, the critique of Marx plays a vital role in their effort to elevate King to revolutionary status because he apparently, unlike Marx, prioritized race in his liberatory project. We addressed Douglas's and Loggins's claims about King in our Conclusion (*The Communist and the Revolutionary Liberal*) and were not persuaded. Not only did King, as Douglas and Loggins themselves instantiate, reject the solution Marx and Engels proposed for ending social inequalities, namely, the abolition of private property, but also the entire programme of the two founders of modern communism and those of their most capable students Lenin and Trotsky.[69]

The most that Douglas and Loggins can say about that rejection is that "King's treatment of Marx was often roughshod, if not disingenuous—a fact owed partly to the pressures put upon him by the Cold War context of the 1950s and early '60s."[70]

But that's apologia. Malcolm X wasn't deterred by that same context from collaborating with communists in his last year. The basic problem with Douglas and Loggins regarding Marx is the same one with Hund, as well as other academic critics: the tendency to treat him in their own self-image, as a scholar. That they reduce him to "the center of his study," rather than to the center of his practice says it all.

What Hund, Douglas, and Loggins all have in common in their critique of Marx is a reliance, to one degree or another, on Cedric J. Robinson's 1983 *Black Marxism: The Making of the Black Radical Tradition*, much more explicitly in the case of the latter two. Robinson's volume was the first book-length indictment of Marx and Engels for their supposed deficit regarding the race question.[71] Owing much to the accolades of historian Robin Kelley, Robinson's critique has gotten the kind of attention that it never had when he was alive.[72] Robinson's solution to Marx's failing, the alternative to their mode of analysis, was the notion of "racial capitalism"—this is what King sought to give content to, according to Douglas and Loggins. Because Robinson never defined "racial capitalism," scholars who have since employed the concept have given their own meaning to it.

This response to Zimmerman, Hund, and Douglas and Loggins is in many ways an update of my 1985 critical review of *Black Marxism*. Some of my above-discussed criticisms of all four were previewed in that essay. Subsequent research permitted me to address in another article (chapter 3 of this book) the all-too-frequent Eurocentric charge against Marx and Engels made, not only by Robinson.[73] Missing in both essays, however, are any of the rich details about Marx and Engels's practice regarding the Civil War—another reason to fault Robinson's book. A revisit to *Black Marxism* reveals what Hund probably has in mind regarding the "debacle for subsequent attempts at a Marxist analysis of racism" and its "effects that are still evident today"—namely, what both Social Democracy and Stalinism did in the names of not only Marx and Engels but of Lenin as well. Much of the target of Robinson's ire is the "opportunism" of both currents, as he calls it, and rightly so; that is, the betrayal of the Black struggle. But to lay those crimes, as Hund and Robinson do, at the feet of Marx and Engels betrays their own theoretical shortcomings when it comes to understanding politics. Lenin and Trotsky remain the best analysts of why those two tendencies fell far short of what Marx's and Engels's original program sought to accomplish.[74]

There is another omission in *Black Marxism*—an almost glaring one. For a book that claimed to be an exposition of the "Black radical tradition," the absence of Malcolm X—less than two decades after his assassination—is remarkable. He didn't even rate a mention in Robinson's list of post–Second World War

Black revolutionaries.[75] That Malcolm X was publicly fraternizing with communists in the last year of his life, white ones to boot, no doubt was a very inconvenient fact for Robinson—his footnotes in *Black Marxism* suggest that he knew about it.[76] Neither, it should be noted, does Frederick Douglass make an appearance in Robinson's account; testimony to the definitional problems with his "Black radical tradition." Was Douglass, the onetime Black slave, not a radical? If not a "Black Marxist," certainly, then at least, as we characterize him, a revolutionary liberal. Had Robinson been truly interested in testing the merits of Marxism against Black political thought, why didn't he even consider what this book does—a return to the foundational moment of Marxism and the best, arguably, that Black political thought then had to offer, which was Douglass—and see what a comparison taught?

The late political philosopher Charles Mills exemplified the academic reading of Marx—almost exclusively at the level of ideas rather than politics. He too, not surprisingly, employed Robinson to charge Marx and Engels with "a clear Eurocentricity in their writings about non-white people."[77] And Mills, to the end, unapologetically defended his apolitical reading—not unlike Robinson—of Marx.[78] Never would it have occurred to him to examine Marx's politics, as we do in this book, to see if his practice informed his ideas about morality, justice and race—all wanting in Marx, according to Mills.[79] "Where is," Mills indignantly once asked, "Karl Marx and Frederick Engels's outraged *Political Economy of Slavery*?"[80] Mills, owing to his earlier embrace of Marxism, likely knew better but by then had consciously chosen not to acknowledge the political Marx—"a missed opportunity," as one scholar aptly puts it, to really engage Marx, to test the validity of his propositions, again, as we do here.[81]

The real world of politics may best explain Mills's subsequent apolitical rendering of Marx, owing to what Hund, as noted earlier, gratuitously faults Marx for—the Social Democratic and Stalinist misrepresentations of Marx's and Engels's project. Those of us who had the good fortune to know Trotsky's explanation of Stalinism were at least theoretically—if not emotionally with regard to the first event—prepared to make sense of the 1985 counterrevolution in the Caribbean nation of Grenada and the collapse, five years later, of the Stalinist regimes in Russia and Eastern Europe.[82] For many, like for Mills, both developments—especially the tragedy in Grenada—were demoralizing and disillusioning. He then sought refuge in the world that the young Marx parted company with. As the two new converts to communism proclaimed in *The German Ideology*, "One has to 'leave philosophy aside' . . . one has to leap out of it and devote oneself like an ordinary man to the study of the actuality, for which there exists also an enormous amount of literary material, unknown, of course, to the philosophers."[83] Whether known or not to him, Mills simply wasn't interested in the rich materials this book has presented to determine if Marx had anything of significance to say about the *Political Economy of Slavery* of "non-white people." Lenin, one might argue, did something similar due to *The Guns of August* of 1914, his deep dive into Hegel to explain Social Democracy's betrayal of proletarian internationalism. But for Lenin that philosophical detour, unlike for Mills, was a means to an end—revolutionary practice.

If Marx and Engels did not have a theory about race, they did have one about social inequality, of which racial oppression is one of its species. That theory was captured all so pedagogically in Engels's question-and-answer number 7 in his final draft that Marx employed to write the *Manifesto*:

> In what way does the proletarian differ from the slave? . . . The slave is sold once and for all, the proletarian has to sell himself by

> the day and by the hour. . . . The slave frees himself by abolishing, among all the private property relationships, only the relationship of slavery and thereby only then himself becomes a proletarian; the proletarian can free himself only by abolishing private property in general.[84]

For Marx and Engels, in other words, private property was the material basis for social inequality and only the proletariat had a class interest *and* capability in ending it and thus ensuring "human emancipation."

Is there any evidence, then, that the fight to end class inequality advances the struggle for racial equality? More specifically, what happens when a society with roots in racial inequality begins to abolish private property? What are the consequences for racial inequality? Again, any evidence? There is, I argue—from our own hemisphere; if not conclusive, certainly suggestive.

Racial slavery has long been the place to begin to explain the persistence of structural or institutional racism—before they came to be called racial capitalism or systemic racism—in societies where the "peculiar institution" was in place. The Western Hemisphere was unique with that iniquitous practice. The three countries where the institution marked the entire societies and prevailed the longest, in that order, are Brazil, Cuba, and the United States, until respectively, 1888, 1884, and 1865. What if we compare outcomes regarding racial inequality for the three countries? What can we learn?

Comparing so different a group of societies is fraught with all kinds of methodological issues, especially, the apples-and-oranges or false equivalency problem. Yet, I argue, there is—to take advantage of a topic on the brains of many as this is being written—something of importance and meaning that can be said with confidence. The probability of someone with visible roots in

Africa losing their life in an encounter with the police is qualitatively greater in, first, Brazil and, second, the United States, than in Cuba. The difference between the first two and the latter is one that did not always exist. Prior to the first of January 1959, the rankings were probably Brazil, Cuba, and the United States in that order without qualitative differences between the three countries. In other words, what a difference a proletarian revolution makes.[85]

What ensued on that historic date was the beginning of the end to all the perks that came with private ownership of the means of production in Cuba, including those of racial privilege. The only way that the Cuban proletariat with roots in Africa could ensure itself of secure employment for the first time was to abolish private property—exactly what the new government that issued from the island-wide general strike on that date began doing, the first time anywhere in the Americas.

What the comparison reveals is that history is not destiny, as proponents of the *New York Times*'s *1619 Project* are prone to believe.[86] How else to explain why Cuba is the outlier of the three societies where racial slavery long existed, if not for its revolution? A detailed comparison for other social indicators such as life expectancy, infant mortality, educational attainment, homelessness would likely yield similar results, and especially if the comparisons are made with Cuba's Caribbean neighbors—Puerto Rico, a colony of the United States, being the most appropriate cohort. The abolition of private property, to wit, has life and death outcomes for the toilers, and especially its most oppressed, as Marx and Engels would have predicted.[87]

What took place in Cuba also had consequences for the worldwide fight against racial oppression—what a theory of race would also have to incorporate. As Nelson Mandela famously remarked when he visited Cuba in 1991, a year and a half after his release from twenty-seven years of prison in South Africa: "The defeat of the racist army at Cuito Cuanavale has made it possible for me to be here today."[88] Largely at the hands of Cuban troops, the South African regime suffered a major military reversal in Angola in 1988 that proved to be critical in ending apartheid—what's possible in the fight against racism when the proletariat has state power.[89]

As the Cuban Revolution has come under increasing pressure from its "neighbor" to the north, world capital's most ardent and effective defender of private property, to carry out "reforms," namely, to grant space to private property, social behaviors that were once rare in revolutionary Cuba have reared their ugly heads. By no means to the degree that it exists ninety miles away but a fact nonetheless—evidence about the inequalities and antisocial values and conduct that come with private property, even with all the limits on it that continue to exist in Cuba. The future of the Cuban Revolution depends on the proletariat elsewhere emulating its example, not the least important being its cohorts to the north. As Engels, again so pedagogically, put it in his last draft that Marx employed for the final document: "Will it be possible for the revolution to take place in one country alone? No . . . the communist revolution will . . . be no merely national one. . . . It is a worldwide revolution and will therefore be worldwide in scope."[90] Little wonder that Washington continues its six-decade-long bipartisan campaign to try to confine the Cuban Revolution to the dustbin of history.

A return to Martin Luther King Jr.'s 1967 epiphany is the appropriate ending for this book's reply to Marx and Engels's critics on the race question. Despite the best efforts of Douglas and Loggins to make him into a revolutionary, most telling is the virtual silence that has since greeted the insight upon which they seek to reinvent him. How to explain why the refrain "I have a dream" is far more likely to be quoted than "a radical redistribution of economic and political power"? For we "class fundamentalists," the answer is elementary. The beneficiaries of the Second Reconstruction—I include myself in that category—now have a class interest in defending private property and this is why they, especially its meritocratic layers, prefer to talk about race rather than class—this is their way to defend recently acquired class privileges. Only the proletariat, to beat the drums again, has a class interest in the abolition of private property. A theory about race that doesn't begin with a theory about class is an ideology, that is, a misrepresentation of social reality.

5

Revisiting *Black Marxism* Four Decades Later: Bringing Marx into the Class-versus-Race Debate

THE NOVEMBER 2024 PRESIDENTIAL ELECTION, it's not an exaggeration to say, put a spotlight on the class versus race debate in U.S. politics like never before. While both campaigns played, in their own ways, the race card, a majority of the voters, *of all colors*, said, as the punditry put it, "It's the economy, stupid." Millions of workers, of all colors, put their stamp on the election by saying "No More" to the Democrats, the so-called friend of labor. This was, for the first time, the necessary, though not sufficient, condition for independent working-class political action in the United States. At the time of this writing, it's too early to say how progressive-minded forces and the left will read and respond to the election results, but the outcome ensures that the decades-long class-versus-race-cum-identity debate is not going away.[1] And for good reason.

Global capitalism's more than half-century-long crisis of

stagnant growth and low productivity—hence, its profitability and accumulation crisis—inevitably breeds social polarization.[2] In the absence, virtually anywhere, of influential, militant working-class parties that actively fight for a program and way forward for the working class to take state power, the crisis also inevitably breeds group consciousness other than that of class consciousness. What the commentariat in the United States simplistically calls "tribal" or "identity" politics speaks to that sobering fact.

Two recent entries in the debate constitute a first: collections of writings of various authors who take one of its two sides. Marc James Léger's ironically titled *Identity Trumps Socialism: The Class and Identity Debate after Neoliberalism* states in its opening paragraph that the "Marxist critique of capitalism" characterizes the writers he has assembled.[3] The second entry, the *Race and Capital* special issue of the journal *Historical Materialism* brings together contributions in the "Marxist tradition."[4] But a close reading of all the articles reveals, except for five paragraphs in one otherwise informative and lengthy essay in the latter collection, that neither Marx nor his partner Engels figures substantively in the arguments of the pro-class side of the debate, particularly its politics.

Marx and Engels's absence, unintentionally gives credence to the claim of the opponents on the "race" side of the debate that the two founders of modern communism didn't have much if anything to say about the matter of identity. Indeed, their frequent complaint is that Marx lacked "a theory of race," or some such variant.[5] The charge, as I've long suspected, is really about Reconstruction, the counterrevolution that brought a bloody end to America's first and brief experiment in racial equality, and the expectation that Marx should have foreseen that outcome.[6]

Is it true that Marx had nothing to say about the race question? Or perhaps nothing that is relevant for today? What if we revisit the moment when he first addressed the topic of race in a sustained way, that is, on the Civil War, or Second American Revolution? And what if we compare, in real-time, Marx's reading and actions to someone who was intimately familiar with and wrote extensively on the topic; someone like, for example, Frederick Douglass, the onetime slave and then freedom fighter—a comparison, therefore, of Marx the communist with the best that revolutionary liberalism has ever offered? Real-time analysis helps to avoid the advantages that come with hindsight—by which any one of us could look smarter than Marx, presuming that he should have anticipated the overthrow of Reconstruction. What might we learn about Marx that retains value? A lot, this essay argues.

The Marx-Douglass comparison is exactly what *The Communist and the Revolutionary Liberal in the Second American Revolution,* co-authored with Kyle Edward, does—some of its key findings summarized here.[7] It's my latest entry in a three-decade-long campaign to bring Marx back to the world he consciously chose to join. His 1844 realist epiphany that "ideas cannot carry out anything at all [and that] men are needed who can exert practical force" enabled his path to communism.[8] Hence his call for "making criticism of politics, participation in politics, and therefore *real struggles,* the starting point of our criticism"—virtually ignored by the standard academic take on Marx.[9] No wonder then the oft-quoted but inadequately absorbed summary thesis of his divorce settlement with the world he was leaving: "Philosophers have only *interpreted* the world, in various ways; the point is to *change* it." Indeed, what Marx then sought to do.

Comparing Marx and Douglass thus permits an update of my 1985 review of Cedric Robinson's *Black Marxism.* His now highly touted book, published in 1983, was, in hindsight, the first sustained retort of those who held that race, rather than class, better explained the continuing oppression of Black Americans despite the legislative gains of what is now called the civil rights movement. The 500-page volume registered how intense—and bloody, in one notorious instance—the debates had been about the still unresolved question.[10] *Black Marxism* has come to be, arguably, the foundational text for opponents of "class fundamentalism" in the now, thankfully, more civil debate. Marx's supposed myopia about the race question, the premise of *Black Marxism*, is a charge to which I'm able, therefore, to make a more informed response than I could in 1985.

Robinson doubled down on his critique of Marx on the race question in the republication of *Black Marxism* in 2000. This doubling down was not in the original 1983 text, as far as I can determine, but rather in the new, extended preface, presumably the intended takeaway of the text two decades after its original publication. After opening with feigned praise for Marx and Engels, he accused them of "deceit" for their "social agenda—in the illusory order and power of pure logic and speculation."

> For Marx, capitalism consisted of a geometric whole whose elementary and often hidden characteristics (price, value, accumulation, and profit) could be discovered with arithmetic means and certainty.
>
> Driven, however, by the need to achieve the scientific elegance and interpretive economy demanded of theory, *Marx consigned race, gender, culture, and history to the dustbin*. . . . Marx's *conceit* was to presume that the theory of historical materialism explained history. . . . Eurocentrism and secular messianism . . . were not the only ideological elements which worked to constrict Marx's imaginary . . . Marx, though he found slavery abhorrent, *similarly recessed slaves from his discourse on human freedom.*[11]

Serious charges. By comparing Marx and Douglass in real-time, during which, as Robinson applauds, "the liberationist agenda of antislavery triumphed," for him a better alternative to Marx's liberatory project, it's possible to determine if they are warranted. Is it true that Marx's historical materialist method handicapped him from being on the right side of history and doing the right thing, thus failing to aid and abet that "antislavery" victory, because he "recessed slaves from his discourse on human freedom"? The findings from my 2024 co-authored book prove just the opposite, and more. The specificity of Robinson's 2000 anti-Marx charges, in other words, lend significance to the Marx-Douglass comparison in a way I was unaware of when I began the project—quantitatively and qualitatively better evidence to refute the key claim of *Black Marxism* than what I offered in my 1985 review of the book.

All too often underappreciated about Marx's project is the prominence in it of the American experience. From the Preface to the very last pages of his magnum opus, *Capital,* that is all so evident. Not coincidentally, I argue, given his political work at the time he wrote much of *Capital.* America's reality figured significantly in his political evolution from a radical democrat, revealing Marx's comparativist instincts—arguably the only scientific way to study social reality.

Marx's very first political writing, at age twenty-four, revealed an awareness about the republic's glaring contradictions, obligating him to praise it for "freedom of the press . . . in its purest most natural form" while condemning slavery—it "can never become lawful, even if it exists a thousand times over as a law"—because it violated "the Negro's human nature."[12] Subsequent research on the "United States of North America" revealed that the state "allows private property, *education,* occupation, to act in their way . . . to exert the influence of their special nature. Far from abolishing these real distinctions, the state only exists on the presupposition of their existence."[13] Nota bene Marx's awareness, long before the SCOTUS 2023 decision about admissions to Harvard, of how "education" in conjunction with "private property" could exert "the influence of their special nature," namely, in perpetuating social inequality. "Political emancipation," therefore, as the world's best example prior to France's Second Republic of 1848, instantiated, should not be mistaken for "human emancipation" or "true democracy." A political system premised on inequality in wealth could never, for the young Marx, be a truly democratic one.

For Douglass, the fundamental problem about America was the "peculiar institution" of slavery making for a "bastard republicanism."[14] For Marx, racial slavery was symptomatic of a deeper problem, a society not only founded on, but one that also privileged private property, thus explaining the hegemony of the wealthiest private property owners in the republic, the "slave traders"— hence, the reason for the "bastard" republic. Something more radical, the young Marx concluded, was needed to bring about "the sovereignty of the people."

Further research on America's peculiar institution taught how the new capitalist mode of production gave an ancient retrograde institution a new lease on life in the first half of the nineteenth century. "Without slavery you have no cotton, without cotton you have no modern industry."[15] Hence, the racial prejudices that accompanied the process—the equation, for example, of blackness with enslavement, with all that implied. As Marx sarcastically retorted in 1847: "What is a Negro slave? A man of the black race. The one explanation is as good as the other." More accurately, he continued, "A Negro is a Negro. Only under certain conditions does he become a slave."[16]

For Douglass, simple "greed" and "selfishness" explained anti-Black "prejudices," whereas for Marx the increasing demand of an insatiable capitalist world market for the product of slave labor that had once been mainly intended for the plantation, the "home market," explained the "greed." In the lead-up to the Civil War, defenders of the slavocracy were unapologetic, as Marx read, about the economic rationale for white supremacy. While it frustrated Douglass, the Christian, to no end that church leaders apologized for slavery, for Marx, the communist, the reason was clear. Years earlier, he had concluded that religion didn't explain anything; rather it was religion that needed to be explained, and the best place to begin was with the social reality in which it was embedded. Despite, however, the then centrality of the "slave-economy" to "modern industry," Marx presciently saw, in 1847, that it "would provoke the most fearful conflicts in the southern states of republican North America."[17]

Europe, where class formation was more developed than in the United States, revealed for Marx and Engels the solution to millennial-old social oppression. A newly emerging class— the proletariat—had not only an inherent class interest in putting an end to the material basis for social inequality, private property, but also the capability to actually do so. Unlike the slave—as Engels explained in the second draft for the *Communist Manifesto*—who could be freed by abolishing only "property in persons," the worker, he posited, could only be freed by abolishing "private property in general."[18] Nothing so distinguished Marx the communist from Douglass the liberal, an adamant opponent of "property in persons" but not "private property in general," as did this most foundational claim of Marx and Engels's "materialist conception of history." Its significance would be on full display after the abolishment of America's peculiar institution.[19]

As long as private property prevailed, the indispensable ingredient for capitalist relations of production, the proletariat's well-being, Marx and Engels discovered, would always be insecure. It depended on whether the owner of property believed that value could be added to it by buying the labor power of someone to do so. Thus, the inherently dependent and precarious reality of being a worker. Hence, why the two authors of the *Manifesto* declared near its end that "Communists" were obligated to "bring to the front, as the leading question in each" of the movements in which they participated in various countries "the property question, no matter what its degree of development at the time." The particular private property that Marx and Engels targeted, as the surrounding and relevant text in the *Manifesto* makes clear, was that of the capitalist, that is, the owner of the means of production.[20]

To repeat, if Marx didn't have "a theory about race," as his critics commonly charge, he did have one about social inequality and how to overcome it. And the dynamics of social exploitation, in which one layer of society lives off the uncompensated labor of another layer of society, went a long way in explaining the variants on a theme such as racial and national oppression. Again, only the proletariat had both a class interest and the capability of putting an end to private property, the material basis for social oppression in general. If that makes us "class fundamentalists," as some charge, we who subscribe to Marx's thesis about what makes the proletariat special—in all of its identities—we plead guilty.

Marx's thesis, by the way, had long historical roots. Two hundred years earlier, Gerard Winstanley, the Digger or True Leveler, declared that class societies and real democracy were incompatible.[21] But the absence of the proletariat in that era made it impossible to envision an effective solution. Ownership of private property, Marx would have argued, is what enabled social oppressors to exercise racist or other such ideologies—without which "a theory about race," however elegant, is woefully insufficient.

Marx and Engels were under no illusion that workers would automatically recognize their need as a class to abolish private property. The word "inevitable," *unvermeidlich* in the original, appears only once in the *Manifesto,* the very last word in Part One. Immediately following in Part Two are instructions about what the working class needed to do to organize itself in order "to raise the proletariat to the position of ruling class, to win the battle of democracy." If a socialist revolution were inevitable, contrary to a lot of supposedly informed opinion, there would have been no need to write the *Manifesto*.

The last section of the document sketches out the tasks for communists in specific countries such as the United States. Though no mention is made of the abolition movement, "the Communists" were expected to work with the National Reform Association, a working-class organization that called for both an agrarian reform and "the abolition of slavery."[22] After describing the tasks for communists in various other countries, there is a summary: "In short, the Communists everywhere support every revolutionary movement against the existing social and political order of things." No directive better anticipated the course of Marx and his comrades on the other side of the Atlantic in the coming years than this one.[23]

Again, for Marx it wasn't enough to have ideas or a theory. Practical and collective political work, organized and disciplined, was necessary for their realization, namely, a political party—which Douglass never participated in, at least prior to and during the Civil War. Marx and his new partner Engels soon began to act on that perspective. Their authorship of the *Manifesto* in 1848, under the direction of a vanguard layer of exiled German workers, registered how quickly they had progressed. Within days of its publication the 1848–1849 revolutions, the European Spring, tested the document's key claims. That two-year revolutionary experience as leaders of the Communist League served them and their comrades well when the second edition of those midcentury upheavals erupted a decade later on the other shore of the Atlantic.

Among the invaluable political takeaways for Marx and Engels about the German version of the European Spring was the critically important need for the working-class movement to be organized independently of bourgeois and petit-bourgeois forces, a requisite that applied as well to the electoral and parliamentary arenas. Elections, the experience taught, should never be seen as an end in themselves but rather an opportunity to do political education and to "count forces" to determine when to make a revolution—the first of three major corrections in the Marx-Engels arsenal, owing to the lessons of "*real struggles*." To believe otherwise about elections was to engage in what the political philosopher Raymond Geuss might call "wishful thinking," what I label "voting fetishism," the mistaken belief that political power is actually exercised in the voting process. And to assume that what took place inside parliamentary walls was the be-all and end-all of politics was to be afflicted with what Marx and Engels called "parliamentary cretinism"—the inspiration for my conceptual innovation.[24]

The slavocracy's fateful attack on Fort Sumter in April 1861 put the liberal and the communist on the same political page—but for different reasons. For Douglass, the conflagration would be an opportunity to end America's "bastard republicanism" and institute "true democracy." For Marx, the overthrow of America's peculiar institution—"the meanest and most shameless form of man's enslaving recorded in the annals of history"—was only, but indispensably, the prelude to "true democracy."[25] Contrary to political philosopher Charles Mills's charge, inspired by Robinson, Marx and Engels were indeed "outraged" by slavery.[26] Putting to bed America's "existing political and social order of things," that is, the slave oligarchy, was the prerequisite for the rule of the proletariat, the grave diggers of class society, enabling "the sovereignty of the people" and thus "human emancipation"—what Marx, in contrast to Douglass, meant by "true democracy."

Douglass had once been a committed pacifist. But the upheavals in Europe in 1848 gave him license to applaud for the first time armed struggle and hence his enthusiasm for the opportunity to use arms to overthrow the Slave Power. They enabled him to be open to John Brown's entreaties to adopt armed struggle, though he wasn't convinced that the attack on Harpers Ferry would actually work. To Douglass's credit, however, he defended Brown's action, arguably the event that did more than any other to put an end to chattel slavery in the United States because it sparked the ill-fated attack on Fort Sumter. Had Robinson been more ecumenical and less a race-exclusionist, he would have included Brown in his pantheon of Black radical tradition figures. Brown's inspiration, more than anyone, was Toussaint L'Ouverture. Brown merits only three in-passing mentions in Robinson's narrative. For Marx, Brown's attack was significant because it would spark a slave uprising. Not the first time that Marx's hopes—in this case, contra Robinson, the abolition of slavery—ran ahead of reality.

Contrary to President Abraham Lincoln's initial pronouncements that the war with the slave oligarchs was only about secession and had nothing to do with the peculiar institution, Douglass and Marx both knew better. More confident than Douglass, Marx proclaimed two weeks into the war that the North would eventually be victorious because of Lincoln's "last card up his sleeve . . . a slave revolution."[27] The experience of having gone through a revolution, though an unsuccessful one, and having battlefield-tested comrades in the Civil War, advantaged Marx and Engels in reading about the American events in the next four years. And their historical materialist perspective—what

Robinson disparages as "conceit"—allowed Marx, from four thousand miles away, to see what Lincoln would eventually have to do: convert the secession war into an abolition war.

Veterans of the European Spring immediately signed on to the Union military project. These included Communist League members, occasionally called "the Marx party," who took the opportunity to continue the fight of 1848–1849 in order to end the "existing political and social order of things," albeit on the other side of the Atlantic. One of them, Joseph Weydemeyer, rose to the rank of lieutenant colonel in the Union Army. From London, Marx did all he could to aid and abet his comrades in America. An invaluable conquest of the 1848 German Revolution is that it made Marx, owing to his prominence as the effective leader of the revolt's most radical wing, an occasional correspondent for the pro-abolitionist *New York Daily Tribune,* the leading daily in the United States.

One of the *Tribune*'s faithful readers happened to be Lincoln—enabling, along with his party comrades, Marx's reach into U.S. politics. His main task was to defend the Union cause against Britain's mostly pro-Confederate organs, mouthpieces for the textile barons who wanted the government to intervene in the war on behalf of the slave oligarchy, upon whom they depended for their slave-produced cotton. Douglass, at the same time, used his eponymous *Monthly* newspaper to criticize the Lincoln administration for not declaring the war to be for abolition. In doing so, Douglass became, intentionally or not, an apologist for Britain's pro-Confederacy "betters" and their organs. Lincoln's stance, in fact, put Marx in the difficult position of trying to make a case for the North, in the face of the president's denials about the purpose of the war.

With the *Tribune* as his podium, Marx decided that his first task was to explain the war's origins. That meant a deep dive into U.S.

history—just as he was beginning to make some headway on his magnum opus, *Capital* (one reason it was never completed)—to understand why the Slave Power emerged and how it operated both economically and politically. Confederate newspapers, he reported, offered convincing evidence that the votes for secession were an elite-driven affair, that of the slave oligarchy. Their documents, especially the speech of Confederate vice president Alexander Stephens, unambiguously revealed that their white supremacy ideology was carefully crafted to serve naked economic self-interest. Class exploitation, in other words, best explained the racist worldview of the slave oligarchs and the war they launched.

If economic gain clearly motivated the slave owners to wage war on the North, less apparent were the reasons for those of the "poor whites," "the plebeians," the non-slaveholding whites in the South who did take up arms on behalf of the slave oligarchs. Why were they willing to do so? Simply because they were infected by the ideology of white supremacy? Marx, in other words, was obligated to address a question that remains as current as ever—why would toilers betray their apparent class interests? Isn't this the issue, in fact, at the heart of today's debate about race and class? "Whither the white proletariat?"

Six months into the war, Marx, on the basis of his research, offered an explanation to *Tribune* readers. While it was clear to many astute observers that the economics of plantation slavery motivated its expansionist drive into non-slaveholding territories, Marx noted a political reason—and not just the need of the slave oligarchy, at the national level, to keep its "political sway over the United States." The only way they could "maintain their sway at home," namely, the South, was "by constantly throwing out to their white plebeians the bait of prospective conquests within and without the frontiers of the United States."[28] Marx returned to this key point a few weeks later in a more didactical way for the liberal Vienna daily, *Die Presse*:

> Only by acquisition and the prospect of acquisition of new Territories, as well as by filibustering expeditions, is it possible to square the interests of these "poor whites" with those of the slaveholders, to give their restless thirst for action a harmless direction and to tame them with the prospect one day of becoming slaveholders themselves.[29]

Southern white toilers, in other words, Marx explained, were willing "to square" or, perhaps, betray their "interests" because of the temptation, "the bait," "the prospect one day of becoming slaveholders themselves."

While Douglass, the onetime slave, personally knew and criticized white toilers who had compromised their class interests by siding with their white bosses, often at the expense of the Black enslaved, he had attributed it only to their anti-Black "prejudices" and their "pride" in being white—the "psychological wage" as W. E. B. Du Bois would later say. For Marx, there was more to their betrayal, specifically, "the prospect," again, of upward mobility. Recent scholarship confirms what Marx detected from four thousand miles away.[30] And for the slave oligarchs, there was another benefit of expanding the peculiar institution westward. Dangling out the "bait" of upward mobility was a way, Marx, the expert analyst of the class struggle, noted "to tame" the potentially unruly "swinish multitude," as they were contemptuously called by the elite.

Northern anti-Black attitudes, registered by the Democratic Party's gains in the 1862 fall elections following the issuance of the Emancipation Proclamation, also elicited an explanation from Marx. "New York City," where the party did well, "strongly corrupted by Irish rabble, actively engaged in the slave trade until recently, the seat of the American money market and full of holders on mortgages on Southern plantations, has always been decidedly 'Democratic,' just as Liverpool is still Tory." Then some elaboration:

> The Irishman sees the Negro as a dangerous competitor. The efficient farmers in Indiana and Ohio hate the Negro almost as much as the slaveholder. He is a symbol, for them, of slavery and the humiliation of the working class, and the Democratic press threatens them daily with a flooding of their territories by "niggers."[31]

Douglass, to be noted, is absent in *Black Marxism*, nary a mention. The reason, I suspect, is that Robinson's race-fundamentalism perspective was never Douglass's lodestar. "Prejudices" is the term Douglass employed to describe anti-Black attitudes among whites. "Racism" only came into vogue in the second decade of the twentieth century as the Google Books Ngram Viewer search engine reveals.

The peculiar institution for Marx—Douglass as well—was the fount for anti-Black attitudes and, thus, why its demise was so very much in the interests of the proletariat. Hence the import of Marx's penultimate paragraph in his congratulatory message, on behalf of the International Workingmen's Association (IWMA), to Lincoln on his reelection in November 1864:

> While the working men, the true political power of the North, allowed slavery to defile their own republic; while before the Negro, mastered and sold without his concurrence, they boasted it the highest prerogative of the white-skinned labourer to sell himself and choose his own master; they were unable to attain the true freedom of labour or to support their European brethren in

> their struggle for emancipation, but this barrier to progress has been swept off by the red sea of civil war.[32]

Racial slavery was the key obstacle to proletarian consciousness and the war that Lincoln was prosecuting therefore deserved support.

Marx reiterated his point in *Capital,* finally published in 1867: "In the United States of North America, every independent movement of the workers was paralyzed so long as slavery disfigured a part of the Republic. Labor cannot emancipate itself in the white skin where in the black it is branded."[33] Again, Marx's premise, too often ignored by his critics, was that only "the working men," namely the proletariat, had an inherent class interest in and capability to end class oppression. Marx, in his congratulatory message to Lincoln, wrote: "The Negro," in their overwhelming majority, were indeed "mastered and sold without his concurrence." Three years later they were still being "branded"—a fact about which Douglass would have been in complete accord. It would take decades, as history showed, before Black toilers became, in their overwhelming majority, members of the proletariat and in a position to exercise the same kind of revolutionary agency.[34]

Douglass, in early 1863, said something strikingly similar at a public talk. Prior to the war,

> the white laborer has been deluded into the belief that to degrade the black laborer is to elevate the white. We shall learn by-and-by that labor will always be degraded where idleness is the badge of respectability. Whence came the degrading phrases, fast growing popular before the war . . . . I think I never saw anywhere such contempt for poor white people as in the South. . . . The war of the Rebels—is a war of the rich against the poor.

Nota bene that for Douglass, the war, continuing into its second year, was about "the rich against the poor," in other words, a class war. But tellingly different from Marx, Douglass assumed that, with the overthrow of chattel slavery, workers would be "paid honest wages for honest work . . . and laborers in all sections of this country rising to respectability and power."[35] Marx had a radically different opinion. What Douglass expected would require the expropriation of "private property in general," the communist solution, something with which the once enslaved would never have agreed.

With leadership responsibilities in the newly organized International Workingmen's Association (IWMA), and trying to complete *Capital,* Marx had no time to formulate a program for post–Civil War America. His priority was writing one for the proletariat worldwide, with the central message that only the working class could liberate itself, the chief lesson of the European Spring and, thus, the need for its own political party.

It fell to Engels to think about the tasks and perspectives for America. His correspondence with Marx party member and now retired Union Army officer Joseph Weydemeyer proved to be invaluable. Two months after the surrender of the Confederacy at Appomattox, Marx expressed alarm at the newly installed Andrew Johnson's administration's attitude toward the former slaves. It "likes me not" he told Engels. "The reaction has already set in in America and will soon be much fortified if the present lackadaisical attitude is not ended *immediately* [my italics]."[36] So much, then, for the Monday morning quarterback critics of Marx who claim that he failed to foresee the counterrevolution that later unfolded.

Engels concurred and pointed to three issues that had to be addressed in order that the situation be turned around: Suffrage for the former slaves, land for them, and the future of the "poor whites."[37] Those were exactly what Weydemeyer took up in three articles in September 1865 for the German-language St. Louis *Westliche Post.* Titled "On the Negro Vote," the articles effectively detailed the Marx party's program for what became known as Reconstruction.[38] Along with the right to vote was the heart of Weydemeyer's proposal: "Why not transfer all the lands that have been abandoned, confiscated, or forfeited through tax default to free Negroes to cultivate independently?" While the "current generation" of "poor whites" could not be counted on, "white craftsmen of the cities" were a better possibility. An alliance of them with the new Black yeomanry constituted Weydemeyer's vision for a new South. Both would be future allies of the "modern worker" in "the great fight between labor and monopolizing capital."

To deny the vote to the newly freed Blacks, Weydemeyer cautioned, "now trained in the use of weapons" was to invite "new disturbances and race wars a la St. Domingo [Haiti]." At the end of September, the IWMA sent a similar message to the "People of the United States," in anticipation of Malcolm X's 1964 speech, "The Ballot or the Bullet," almost a century later. Not only could Marx envision a counterrevolution, but so too could the leading Marx party member in America and the Marx party, the organization he now effectively headed. Most instructive, both sought to do what they could to make sure that such an outcome would not be inevitable.

Douglass would have been on board with Weydemeyer on the suffrage issue—he had been saying as much for almost two years—and probably the same with regard to the "poor whites." Not so, however, when it came to Weydemeyer's land proposals. Douglass, the former slave, adamantly opposed property in persons but, like most Republicans, fiercely defended "private property in general." So, when Radical Republican Thaddeus Stevens made a similar land proposal in 1865, Douglass was deafeningly silent. Engels, informed by the key point in his 1847 final draft for the *Manifesto*, namely, the difference between the slave and the proletarian regarding the property question, would not have been surprised about Douglass's non-support for Stevens's proposal. The failure of the Stevens plan to get any traction with fellow Republicans spelled, in hindsight, the beginning of the end to the promise of Reconstruction.

The movement of the "modern worker" in the United States that Weydemeyer looked to was too immature to offer the leadership that would have made Reconstruction successful. Black toilers also lacked a leadership that could have facilitated an alliance with proletarian fighters to do the same. A telling example of what was missing was the Great Railroad strike of 1877. It "brought together 'white and colored men . . . men of all nationalities in one supreme contest for the common rights of workingmen,'" according to one contemporary account.[39] Though heartened by this strike, Marx remained sober. The strike, he said in a letter to Engels, "will, of course, be suppressed" given its leadership deficit, but suggested what it portended—a fighting alliance of Black and white toilers and the possible founding of "a serious workers' party in the United States."[40]

Such an outcome is just what the post–Civil War American ruling class wanted to avoid. With the blessing of Northern capital and its institutions like the Supreme Court, the former slave oligarchs were able to erect the Jim Crow regime, a variant, as Marx noted on occasion, on the millennial-long tactic of *divide et impera*. Two centuries earlier, ruling elites in colonial Virginia instituted the first edition of a ruling-class solution to a multiracial plebeian rebellion, Nathaniel Bacon's Revolt in 1675–1676. Contrary to the claims of the *New York Times*'s *1619 Project*, America's "original sin," namely, racial slavery, began not in that year but rather in the aftermath of Bacon's revolt.[41]

Decades later Douglass came close to regretting his, and the failure of other Republicans, to support Thaddeus Stevens's land proposals—when it was too late. "Our reconstruction measures were radically defective. They left the former slave completely in the power of the old master."[42] This was precisely why Weydemeyer the communist called for the confiscation of the lands of the former slave oligarchs; to deny them their power, namely, their private property. Conversely, Douglass, one of the "field hands" for the Republican Party, as he once described himself and other faithful Black party members, was politically incapable of subscribing to such a proposal.[43]

Like other Republicans, Douglass suffered from "voting fetishism." Stevens, like Marx party member Weydemeyer, knew better. So too did onetime slave owner but Union supporter Charles Hopkins. His prescience was on display in a November 1865 interview: "Civil rights are good for nothing, the ballot is good for nothing, till you make men of every class landholders."[44] Worth noting here are remarks that Martin Luther King Jr. made days before his assassination, in 1968: "In 1863 the Negro was told that he was free as a result of the Emancipation Proclamation being signed by Abraham Lincoln. But he was not given any land to make that freedom meaningful."[45] Therein, for King, the origin of the racial inequality that Black people then faced—and continue to face.

When the Democrats, supporters of Andrew Johnson, suffered major losses in the fall 1866 elections, Marx read it as a sign that the "workers in the North have at last fully understood that white labour will never be emancipated so long as black labour is still stigmatised"—a point he repeated in *Capital* a year later.[46] History proved Marx to have been overly optimistic about "white labor" in the immediate aftermath of the Civil War. Only after the Second Reconstruction in the next century would that hope begin to be fulfilled. The last pages of his magnum opus were more accurate about the future. The logic of capitalist relations of production would inevitably produce a hereditary proletariat in the United States for the first time, the sine qua non, as it turned out, for what the Second Reconstruction was able to achieve.

The American experience offered lessons for Marx about another example of what he and Engels called "stigmatizing" or "branding," specifically, that of the Irish. The use of anti-Irish prejudices—as Douglass also noted—was effectively employed by Britain's elites to divide English and Irish workers, not unlike how anti-Black attitudes functioned in a similar way in both the South and the North to divide Black and white toilers. But more consequential, Marx rethought his prior position about the Irish struggle for national self-determination, his second major self-correction.[47] That revision on Marx's part prepared his followers in the United States a century later to recognize the revolutionary significance of Black nationalism when it appeared and lend it their support.

The Paris Commune—the rebellion of the Parisian proletariat in March 1871 and establishment of a revolutionary government in the French capital—alarmed ruling elites in the United States. Their fear that it might be emulated by former slaves in alliance with an increasingly mobilized white proletariat convinced them to pull the plug on Reconstruction, the final nail in its coffin.[48] The title of Marx's homage to the Communards, *The Civil War in France,* evidenced how much America's conflagration had impacted him. The inability of the Commune to do something truly transformative in France prompted Marx and his partner to make another political correction. The insurgent proletariat "learned on its own," Marx emphasized, that "the working class cannot simply lay hold of the ready-made state machinery and wield it for its own purposes"—an uncertainty in Marx's prior analysis of the state.[49] Socialist transformation, in other words, required a new state form. The bloody counterrevolution that ended the two months of plebeian rule in Paris foreshadowed the bloody end of America's Second Revolution. But the Commune's lessons, distilled in Marx's paean, came to be Lenin's lodestar and, hence, enormously consequential.[50]

Marx, who died in 1883, didn't live long enough to see the full demise of America's brief experiment in racial equality. Engels, who died in 1895, lived to see that it was at best on life-support. His 1893 letter to Marx party leader Frederick Sorge sought to explain why the American proletariat had yet to establish its own political party, unlike what its cohorts in Europe were then doing, instituting mass working-class parties for the first time. Three obstacles, he wrote, stood in the way of doing the same. First, an electoral system whose rules made it difficult for third parties to get off the ground; second, the absence, as yet, of a hereditary working class in America, due largely to the availability of land, that is, the American dream of upward mobility was still real; and third, the divisions within the working class, not the least "the Negro question." Still, Engels remained optimistic that developments were underway in the United States that would make it possible, one day, for there to be "a socialist labour party" in the country.[51]

Three years later "the Negro question" would be more prominent than ever when the Supreme Court sanctioned racial segregation, in 1896, thus giving its official imprimatur in *Plessy v. Ferguson* to Jim Crow, the regime of white supremacy. It would take five decades for the infamous decision to be overturned, in 1954, when the Supreme Court ruled against segregation in *Brown v. Board of Education*. By then, a hereditary American proletariat was in place for the first time—the only class, to repeat, that had not only a class interest but also the capability of ending social inequality and thus making the realization of racial equality a possibility for the first time.

Because Marx and Engels didn't live to see the counterrevolution in all its dimensions, it fell to their political progeny to explain the demise of Reconstruction—exactly what W. E. B. Du Bois did in 1935, in his magisterial *Black Reconstruction*. Both before its publication and in the volume itself, he made clear that the kernels of wisdom that Marx had left inspired his most accomplished project.[52]

At the heart of the volume, at least for purposes here, is the argument in Du Bois's appropriately titled chapter 14, "Counter-Revolution of Property." So persuasive is his Marxist-inspired thesis that even a *New York Times* columnist can now openly promote it. "Why I keep coming back to Reconstruction," the title of Jamelle Bouie's October 25, 2022, essay, argues that it was precisely, as Du Bois demonstrated, "the 'counterrevolution of property' North and South" that "killed Reconstruction" and "not race and culture calling out in the South in 1876." This stands in glaring contrast to the *Times*'s much promoted *1619 Project*, which argues the opposite, namely that white supremacy is the culprit for Reconstruction's demise.[53] The "reason," Bouie concludes,

> I keep coming back to "Black Reconstruction" is that Du Bois's mode of analysis can help us (or, at least, me) look past so much of the ephemera of our politics to focus on what matters most: the roles of power, privilege and, most important, capital in shaping our political order and structuring our conflicts with one another.[54]

Though Bouie doesn't acknowledge the Marxist origins of Du Bois's argument, it serves, nevertheless, to render moot Wulf

Hund's complaint about Marx not having bequeathed "a theory of race" (discussed in chapter 4). Hund's real issue is his disagreement with Marx's class-based explanation of race-cum-social inequality. *Black Marxism* figures prominently in Hund's anti-Marx tract—it's inspiration, I argue.

Nothing, therefore—to return to the point that initiates this essay—could be further from the truth than Robinson's charge that Marx "recessed slaves from his discourse on human freedom." Just the opposite. This is why Marx could be on the same abolitionist page with Douglass for four years, fighting for the same goal—not, as for Douglass, an end, but rather as a means to an end. Only with the overthrow of chattel slavery could the full development of a hereditary proletariat in the United States be ensured for the first time—the only class that had not only the interest but also the capacity to end class society, the requisite for "human freedom."

If Marx's critics find his thesis about the proletariat and its unique liberatory capacity unconvincing, they should say so. More important, they should let us know if they have a better candidate, a better agent for human emancipation. Otherwise, their criticism is made from the position of, if I may, class privilege—those who have found a comfortable niche in the capitalist order by being sideline critics or Monday morning quarterbacks, and who feel no need to offer an alternative perspective.

So What? Lessons for Today?

Do the conclusions that Marx and Engels drew from "making criticism of politics, participation in politics and therefore *real struggles*," particularly, those in the United States, have currency? Are they useful in advancing the nation's unfinished fight against, specifically, racial oppression? But why single out America and its racial conundrum? Surely there are other countries that would qualify for attention. Simply and soberly because that's where the weapons that will likely determine the future existence of our species are stored. The hands that they finally end up in, which class, to be exact, will be decisive. That's not an alarmist claim in the era of Trump. What follows can be at best only a beginning for something more comprehensive.

In his final years Martin Luther King Jr. grappled with a dilemma; how to explain why the legislative conquests of the civil rights movement, the 1964 Civil Rights Act and the 1965 Voting Rights Act, were not likely to end racial disparities in America, soberly evidenced by the urban rebellions in the North where Blacks, unlike their kindred in the South, had, in both theory and fact, enjoyed the right to vote for decades. About a year or more before his assassination in April 1968, MLK had an epiphany: racial equality in the United States would require "a radical redistribution of economic and political power." King, tragically, didn't live long enough to spell out the content of that revelation. But the achievement of anything like that, in its ordinary meaning, would have effectively put an end to the capitalist mode of production that reigns in the United States. Was that ever a real option in 1968? Historical perspective, once again, to the rescue.

Engels, as noted earlier, opined in 1893 on the prospects for socialism in America and pointed to three obstacles: the electoral system, "the American Dream," and working-class divisions, especially the subjugation of African Americans. Nevertheless, to repeat, Engels was optimistic about the long run, the eventual construction of an American "socialist workers party." Informing that optimism was Marx's prediction, at the very end of *Capital*, his magnum opus. The logic of capital, he argued, would make self-employed producers an endangered species in the United

States, to be replaced by a hereditary proletariat with all the precarity and potential of that reality.

How accurate were Engels and Marx's insights and predictions about the United States? Let's begin with "the American Dream." The Great Depression of the 1930s and the exponential growth of the labor movement as a result registered, for the first time, the existence of a hereditary American proletariat. Self-employed producers, as Marx had predicted, were now outnumbered by wage workers. Four decades later, the two recessions of the mid-1970s and the early 1980s signaled the end to the post–Second World War capitalist boom, the end of "the American Century." The Great Recession of 2008 and its continuing repercussions are simply the most recent manifestation of what ails capitalism, the decades-long phenomena of stagnant economic growth and low productivity with all the accompanying consequences. The best that capitalism has to offer the working class is behind us. Arguably, the best evidence for this is the grim news of the deteriorating life expectancy rates for workers in "white skin," now called "deaths of despair."[55]

The Trump phenomenon, I contend, attests better than anything to the validity of Marx's claims about the logic of capital, dismissed by Robinson as "conceit." His MAGA movement is precisely the product of capitalism's inability to deliver "the Dream" to increasing numbers of American workers. The day before Trump's election, on November 5, 2024, workers at Boeing voted unsuccessfully to restore the pensions that their bosses took away a decade earlier—the reality for the American proletariat, in all its skin colors. Boeing workers had been among the best paid in the United States, having once enjoyed benefits like pensions, the working-class ticket to the middle class.[56] Again, that's behind us.[57]

The unprecedented crisis of capitalism is the necessary starting point to answer the question "Whither the white proletariat?"—the real question for skeptics like Robinson of Marx's project. When Marx first posed the "poor white" question; specifically, why were poor whites willing "to square" their class interests with the slave owners who treated them with contempt, he offered an answer: "the bait." That is, "the prospect one day of becoming slaveholders themselves." That answer, I argue, works well in explaining why a worker in "white skin" both then and now might be willing to betray their class interests—the possibility of upward mobility.

Marx complemented the point with an astute observation about Northern white workers in his congratulatory message to Lincoln upon his reelection in 1864: "While before the Negro, mastered and sold without his concurrence, they boasted it the highest prerogative of the white-skinned laborer to sell himself and choose his own master; they were unable to attain the true freedom of labor."[58] As long as white workers thought they were better off than the enslaved, what Du Bois later called the "psychological wage" of whiteness, they were willing to tolerate the rule of capital and thus their own condition as wage slaves.

Most workers today, regardless of skin color or any other identity, are all too familiar with the boss or supervisor who tempts them with perks or the possibility of perks to undermine solidarity with their co-workers. And the precarity that comes with being a worker makes all of them susceptible to such temptations. Class betrayal, class collaborationism, "false class consciousness," etc., are not, therefore, peculiar to any one group of workers. More determinant are the resources available to the bosses to effectively entice a particular group of workers. The more than half-century-old crisis of capitalism reveals diminishing opportunities for achieving "the American dream." The Black proletariat in cities like Gary, Indiana, and Baltimore, Maryland, were the canaries in the coal mine for the so-called deindustrialization process that came with the recessions in the 1970s and 1980s in the last century. All the now hollowed-out towns and cities in the so-called Rust Belt testify to the profundity of the crisis. There were not enough Black bodies to absorb it and thus shield the white proletariat from the lawful workings of the capitalist mode of production.

Trump, with success, has demagogically exploited that misery. Engels's 1881 insight is apropos as I write: "A drowning man clutches at any straw, nor can he wait for the boat to push off from the bank and come to his rescue. The boat is socialist revolution, the straw, protective tariffs and state socialism."[59] Decisive in Trump's first victory were the 209 counties in the Rust Belt that voted for him, counties whose electorates had voted twice for Obama. Can one confidently say that racism motivated their votes for Trump? Might not disappointment with Obama, a Democrat, be a more credible explanation? As in the case, perhaps, of Ashli Babbitt, the January 6, 2021, protester killed by the Capitol Hill police, who "votes for Obama twice, [and] thinks he's the best president ever."[60]

That there are fewer perks today to tempt workers to betray their class interests is no guarantee that they will not do so. The only effective resistance to the "bait" of the bosses is conscious leadership, on both the shop floor and beyond. "Inevitable"appears only once in the *Communist Manifesto*, immediately followed by declarations as to the way the working class can defend itself, namely only through solidarity. Trade unions, the elementary organizational tool of workers, and, most importantly, workers' own political parties—whose nonexistence so far exacts an enormous toll on the American working class—are indispensable. The two-hundred-year history of the class struggle has demonstrated that a communist vanguard is also needed, especially for that most important moment, when the proletariat decides to take state power, "to win the battle for democracy" as the *Manifesto* puts it. Because, as Lenin, Marx's most capable student, so presciently put it in 1901, "It is too late to form the organization in times of explosion and outbursts."[61] Think about the Arab Spring, a tragic confirmation of that insight.

If the American Dream has increasingly become an American nightmare for many workers in all skin colors, what about "the Negro question"? What has and has not changed since Engels raised the issue?

Because "labor in black skin" was still "branded," in the language Marx employed—to wit, the Jim Crow regime—the working-class radicalization of the 1930s was limited in its degree of class consciousness. For that to change, a Second Reconstruction was required. Unlike the first one, the Black working class was able to put its stamp on the second one—what Malcolm X represented. His constant refrain of being a "field slave" as opposed to being a "house slave," his characterization of the Black middle-class leadership, was a conscious appeal to the Black masses. For good reason. The overwhelmingly proletarian composition of the civil rights movement goes a long way toward explaining its success—the missing ingredient in the failed First Reconstruction.

Nothing in recent history registers better what the Second Reconstruction was able to accomplish than the George Floyd protests in 2020—which I had the privilege to participate in, in fact, the very first one.[62] Exactly a century earlier, in the state where the police murdered Floyd, three Black men were brutally lynched and ten thousand white Minnesotans celebrated the atrocity, with many getting their pictures taken among the broken and mutilated bodies.[63] A century later, thousands of Minnesotans of the same skin color—some, no doubt, descendants of the earlier celebrants—marched to denounce Floyd's murder. Before the twenty-first century, anti-police protests had been an almost all-Black affair—probably what I uniquely knew among the other five thousand, mostly youthful and white, protesters in Minneapolis on May 25, 2020. At one time in the country's not too distant past, it could be life-threatening, to be white and in proximity to such protests, as a very ugly incident during the Rodney King protests in Los Angeles in 1992 harrowingly demonstrated.[64]

How to explain the change? About midway between both sets of murders in Minnesota, 1920 and 2020, the national mostly Black proletarian mass movement had won the respect of tens of millions of white working-class Americans; enough to cause them to begin to rethink the "branding of labor in black skin." The United States, as a result, is less racist and more tolerant than it has ever been. Not to recognize that fact is to fail to see the opportunities that exist in America today to do something far more emancipatory than ever—not the least of which to do transracial political work that fighters before us on whose shoulders we stand would have died for.

What about the claim that the Trump ascendancy constitutes a counterrevolution, an overthrow of the historical gains America made on the race question due to the civil rights movement? The *New York Times*'s *1619 Project* originates in that mistaken and dangerous contention and hence is given its resources, its most influential advocate. The *Project* complements the proponents of critical race theory who charge that the institution of chattel slavery implanted "systemic racism" into the nation's DNA, a disease from which it can never escape.

Parliamentary cretinism and voting fetishism fueled the unrealistic expectations that came with the Obama presidency, the widely held but mistaken belief that something of fundamental import had come with his election in 2008. Rather than installing a new operating system, as I sometimes put it, the electorate had simply downloaded a new app with lots of bells and whistles. The Trayvon Martin murder in 2012, which birthed the Black Lives Matter movement, and the exoneration of his killer was probably the back-to-reality moment for most people. With the election of Trump four years later it was easy to subscribe to the thesis of white supremacy triumphant and the concomitant belief that the Second Reconstruction had either been a phantasm or had gone down to defeat like its predecessor after the Civil War.[65] Not knowing of or forgetting about King's epiphany in his last year was, therefore, glaringly on display. To repeat, there could never be racial equality in America, King admitted, "until there is a radical redistribution of economic and political power"—what the electoral/parliamentary process under capitalist relations of production can never deliver.

Yes, systemic racism is real—it's called capitalism; it can't be otherwise.[66] Never have there been better conditions in America for forging the kind of transracial working-class alliance necessary for putting capitalism to rest. The best of the George Floyd moment is indisputable evidence. The white jurors in the three highest-profile cases of that moment, the murders of Floyd, Daunte Wright, and Ahmaud Arbery, who voted to convict, not just other whites but white cops for killing Black people, testified to how much had changed in America.[67] Those convictions, unprecedented in the country's history, are an inconvenient, and still largely unacknowledged, fact for those who contend that Trump's ascent constituted white supremacy redux. Not to be ignored, also, is that Trump's 2020 reelection campaign sought to stoke "white backlash" to the burning and looting in the wake of Floyd's murder. Richard Nixon successfully employed that strategy— "law and order" being a central campaign slogan—in the 1968 presidential election. A half-century later, it didn't work.

With African Americans becoming political citizens for the

first time, the potential now exists for doing something far more liberating as Marx and Engels once envisioned—"the abolition of property in general," as Engels once put it so didactically, the prerequisite for the end to capitalism and, thus, class society.

Though we'll never know for sure, it's unlikely that King—like Frederick Douglass a century earlier—would have opted for or acted to bring about "a radical redistribution of economic and political power." Most likely, he would have opposed it. His Black preacher-style, back-and-forth with an audience in 1967 at the historic Ebenezer Baptist Church in Atlanta, nine months before his assassination, made clear what that epiphany *did not* mean:

> Now, don't think you have me in a bind today. I'm not talking about communism. What I'm talking about is far beyond communism. (Yeah) My inspiration didn't come from Karl Marx (Speak); my inspiration didn't come from Engels; my inspiration didn't come from Trotsky; my inspiration didn't come from Lenin. Yes, I read [the] *Communist Manifesto* and *Das Kapital* a long time ago (Well), and I saw that maybe Marx didn't follow Hegel enough. (All right) He took his dialectics, but he left out his idealism and his spiritualism. And he went over to a German philosopher by the name of Feuerbach, and took his materialism and made it into a system that he called "dialectical materialism." (Speak) I have to reject that.[68]

King, in other words, consciously rejected the course that Marx and Engels advanced.

If not a Marxist, then how to characterize King's politics? Sympathetic accounts claim that he saw himself as a "democratic socialist."[69] That's probably true. While critical of capitalism, as King was occasionally, never did twentieth-century social democracy, which democratic socialists in the United States essentially embrace, act to abolish "private property in general." Rather than call for the overthrow of capitalism, King, like social democrats, sought to reform it. The capitalist state, in his view, could be employed to bring about racial equality. While King certainly pursued mass protests to advance that struggle, he too, like social democrats, viewed the legislative and electoral arenas as being ultimately more consequential in that quest. His decision in 1964 to suspend the protests in order to ensure the election of Democratic Party nominee Lyndon Johnson to the presidency—so different from the stance that Malcolm X took—is exemplary.

To the American Psychological Association annual meeting in September 1967, King cited political science findings suggesting that voting would not be the panacea for racial equality. But if they were right, King responded, then "the main thrust of Negro effort has been, and remains, substantially irrelevant; we may be facing an agonizing crisis of tactical theory."[70] None of the authors of that research, as far I've been able to determine, ever thought it important—telling about the political science discipline, at least in that era—to respond to King's complaint.[71]

But Marx and Engels could have told King as much, given the lessons of 1848–1849 about the reality of the parliamentary and electoral arenas—the inability of either to realize fundamental change. They could have warned him about the fate of those who also thought that the bourgeois state could be employed for the "radical redistribution of economic and political power." The many social democratic corpses that litter the political highway since the Paris Commune—most recently, the Syriza Party in Greece—instantiate that claim.

In contrast to King, Malcolm X offers rich lessons. Within a few years of making it onto the cover of *Time* magazine for the first time, 1957, King encountered a challenge to his leadership of the Black population. From the end of the Civil War in 1865 until his death in 1895, Douglass, the King of his era, successfully fended off rivals. But, by 1960, Malcolm X, a minister in the once obscure Nation of Islam, effectively appeared as a conscious rival to King, especially in Northern working-class Black communities. Back in Douglass's era, the absence of a hereditary Black proletariat was what allowed Douglass and his Black middle-class / private-property / Republican Party orientation to be hegemonic for so long in Black America. King had no such luck. Unlike King, Malcolm X, a onetime factory assembly-line worker—from and of the proletariat in Black skin—was the product of the great migration of the former debt-slave sharecroppers northward, after both twentieth-century world wars, into the working class.

Malcolm X's unwavering Black nationalism—self-determination for Black people—repulsed most who called themselves communists, particularly those in the Communist Party USA (CPUSA). What Malcolm promoted, in their opinion, was Black anti-white sentiment, therefore making it difficult, if not impossible, to realize transracial working-class unity. There is no evidence that the Party has ever rethought its rejection of Malcolm X. In fact, the origin of the post–Second World War class-versus-race debate lies in the challenge faced by those who favored class struggle as to how best to respond to Malcolm X's nationalism. For those of us who lived politically at that moment, and were sympathetic to a class perspective, there was no obvious answer.

The U.S. Socialist Workers Party (SWP) proved to be the notable exception to the mostly negative response of Marxist currents to Malcolm X. Proponents of the King-as-revolutionary thesis, Andrew Douglas and Jared Loggins, attribute King's rejection of Marxism "partly to the pressures put upon him by the Cold War context of the 1950s and early 60s."[72] But 1964–1965 is exactly the moment when Malcolm X openly fraternized with the SWP—white communists to boot. He spoke at their public forums, made himself available for their interviews, and endorsed their newspaper. His proletarian roots, unlike King's middle-class upbringing, most likely facilitated that collaboration. So much, then, for the CPUSA's charge that Malcolm X hated white people or the dubious theory that he and King were on a political convergence course.[73]

Unlike for King, a credible case can be made that Malcolm X was indeed on a convergence course with communism at the end of his life.[74] That would explain the remarkable absence at the end of *Black Marxism* of Malcolm X in the list of names of the leading post–Second World War figures in the "Black radical tradition" (what I failed to notice in my 1985 reading of the book).[75] The Malcolm X-SWP collaboration in the last thirteen months of Malcolm's life constituted, I suspect, a most inconvenient fact for Robinson. It challenged his basic claim of there being an inherent incompatibility between those who subscribe to the political primacy of class and those who uncompromisingly fight for the liberation of oppressed nationalities. Marx and his most capable students knew better.

Malcolm X was the lone leading Black figure during the 1964 presidential campaign who did not subscribe to supporting the lesser-evil Democratic Party candidate, Lyndon Johnson. His position that "we won't organize any Black man to be a Democrat or a Republican because both of them have sold us out. Both parties are racist, and the Democratic Party is more racist than the Republican Party," no doubt was key in getting the attention of the SWP. Malcolm's perceptive insight, after the election in which Democratic candidate Lyndon Johnson defeated Republican candidate Barry Goldwater was: "The shrewd imperialists knew that the only way people would run toward the fox would be if you showed them the wolf."[76]

Ten days before his assassination in February 1965, Malcolm

X, when asked by the Guyanese writer and activist Jan Carew, "aren't you [a Marxist]?", responded:

> I'm a Muslim and a revolutionary, and I'm learning more and more about political theories as the months go by. The only Marxist group in America that offered me a platform was the Socialist Workers Party. I respect them and they respect me. The Communists have nixed me, gone out of their way to attack me . . . that is, with the exception of the Cuban Communists. If a mixture of nationalism and Marxism makes the Cubans fight the way they do and makes the Vietnamese stand up so resolutely to the might of America and its European and other lapdogs, then there must be something to it.[77]

No wonder that Robinson could never include Malcolm X in the "Black radical tradition." The Malcolm X-SWP collaboration and convergence owes itself, as I argued in the preceding chapter, to the consequential correction that Marx made on the Irish question in 1869 and bequeathed to Lenin. The conditions that made the collaboration possible are more extant than ever—the ever-deepening crisis of capitalism—and thus there's no reason to assume it will not reappear in one form or another.

If Marx and Engels were right about the eventual birth of a hereditary proletariat in the United States, and if "the Negro question" has now been answered with a Second Reconstruction—political citizenship for the first time—what about Engels's *longue durée* optimism for an American working-class party? The *longue durée* has proven to be longer than Engels might have imagined.

The biggest challenge that progressive forces face in the United States is not the issue of race but rather how to deal with the Democratic Party, the historic graveyard of progressive movements.[78] As well as the two related problems of lesser-evil thinking and voting fetishism—issues that Marx, Engels, and Douglass had to grapple with, offering, in so doing, invaluable lessons for today. "Trump-the-existential-threat-to-democracy," the Democratic Party's slogan for the 2024 election, tested the political acumen of progressives once again, just as its "Goldwater-the-existential-threat-to-humanity" slogan did in 1964. That they largely succumbed, once again, to its siren call reveals that Malcolm X's clarity and example regarding independent working-class politics are needed more than ever.

When I first encountered the Impeach Bush movement in 2007, I had to think about how to respond pedagogically and nonsectarian-like.[79] Eventually, I found an effective response. "If we don't," I said, "impeach the system that gave us Bush, we'll have someone in the White House who'll make us long for him." No, I didn't have a crystal ball that foresaw the Donald Trump presidency; only the lessons distilled by Marx, Engels, and Lenin. Today, I confidently say that if we don't impeach the system that's given us Trump 2.0, we'll have someone in the White House who'll make us long for, yes, Trump. No, he's not the worst that capitalism has in store if need be, to save its system. Think, for example, of Tucker Carlson, who consciously courts the American working class—not unlike how National Socialism once courted the German working class.

Every delay, every excuse for voting for another lesser-evil Democrat and not doing the hard but necessary work of constructing a party that truly represents the interests of the proletariat for the first time in America, one based on its rank-and-file institutions, trade unions, makes such a chilling outcome more probable. The decades-long retreat of the working class is behind us, as witnessed by the willingness of workers in recent years to take by the tens of thousands to the picket lines again.[80] Never has an electorate been so turned off by the choices the two capitalist parties offer for election—why millions of workers of all skin colors said No to the Democrats. That fact, in combination with an increasingly militant working class, makes for conditions more propitious than ever in initiating independent working-class political action—the prerequisite for doing something truly transformational in American politics.[81]

The distance between what I wrote about Robinson's *Black Marxism* in 1985 and the accolades that have been poured on Cedric Robinson and his book since then is a sobering indicator of what was lost with the assassination of Malcolm X—a measure of the generational break in the Black struggle. Those of us who were radicalized by his example and that of the Cuban Revolution had, fortunately, a high bar against which to measure anything that claimed to be revolutionary. *Black Marxism*, it soon became clear, didn't meet the standard set by both. Not only inadequate, but Robinson's book also constituted an actual retreat from the revolutionary project, a return to a world where Malcolm had once been—the metaphysical one and why he eventually broke with the Nation of Islam. His retreat allowed Robinson to treat "the world's Black peoples" as an undifferentiated, classless world, with all the political pitfalls that came with such blinders—the reason why African revolutionaries grounded in reality solicited my critical review of the book. No wonder that Malcolm's name doesn't appear on Robinson's list of notables in the "Black radical tradition."

More problematic in *Black Marxism* is the absence of another figure and event on its pages, even more telling than Malcolm X's missing name. I made brief mention of it at the end of my 1985 review but could not fully see its significance, too close in time to be able to do so.[82] Incontestably, the apotheosis of the diasporic Black revolutionary tradition—from the Haitian Revolution until now—is what took place on the leeward Caribbean island of Grenada between 1979 and 1983—exactly when Robinson was writing his book.

The Grenada Revolution, led by Maurice Bishop and his New Jewel Movement, constitutes, despite being overthrown by a Stalinist counterrevolution, the most authentic Black proletarian revolution to date.[83] It is exactly for that reason that, like Malcolm X's name, it was ignored by Robinson—another inconvenient fact for a cultural nationalist like him. Rather than recognize facts that challenge his idealist worldview, Robinson chose to erase them. Those of us still alive who had the privilege to witness and, importantly, defend Grenada's Revolution are obligated to let subsequent generations know about Robinson's telling omission.[84]

Robinson's decision to label his project "Black Marxism" registered how much those of us who subscribe to the authentic Marx had achieved. As a cultural nationalist, Robinson was obligated at least to dress as a "Marxist" by claiming to be more critical of capitalism than Marx himself, who, Robinson charged, never saw or understood the significance of race—something a comparison of Marx and Douglass indisputably refutes.

Robinson's anti-capitalist nod, what he calls "racial capitalism," provides a potential opening for education about the real Marx. But there is nothing inherently anti-capitalist about the identity of race—just ask Barack Obama—or other identities such as gender, etc. It's not enough to be against capitalism: more important, what are you for and how do you achieve it? Only the working class, to repeat for the umpteenth time, has an inherent class interest in ending capitalism, because only with the end of private property—the bedrock of capitalism—can the proletariat be liberated.

Private property, as the history of class society has taught for the last ten millennia, is the material basis for social inequality of any variety. Only an alliance of workers in all their various identities, as Marx and Engels explained, can put an end to capitalism—in the spirit of "workers of the world unite." Robinson consciously rejected that perspective, and to employ him, especially today, handicaps its users for explaining class politics, including that of "the world's Black peoples." Keeanga Yamahtta-Taylor is correct about the limitations of Robinson's notion of "racial capitalism."[85] But it is the absence of any sense of the class struggle in his *Black Marxism* that is the bigger problem.

Not for naught, to repeat, did I end my 1985 review with the comradely advice of Grenada's Maurice Bishop in 1983 to antiracist fighters in the United States:

> [I] . . . would very strongly recommend to the Black movement in America the importance of developing the firmest and closest links with the white working-class movement and the white progressive movement. Our feeling certainly is that in order to win that struggle inside of America, it's extremely important that all progressive forces get together and wage a consistent fight against the real enemy.[86]

Advice that is even more apropos today, given the end of the American Dream for most "workers in white skin," which hadn't yet ended when Bishop made the recommendation.

Therein is the likely explanation for the initial neglect of *Black Marxism*. Bishop's advice was informed by a moment of revolutionary optimism on a global scale. Grenada's revolution in 1979 was accompanied by two others that year, the Sandinista triumph in Nicaragua and the overthrow of the Shah, Washington's loyal agent in the Middle East, by the workers and peasants of Iran. Nothing in Robinson's 1983 tome resonated with that development. *Black Marxism* constituted, rather, a retreat to the past, concerning itself with only one component of humanity, "the Black world," as if it constituted an undifferentiated entity.

Therein lies the reason for the later appeal of Robinson's book. Once the 1979 global revolutionary moment had ebbed, beginning, in the eyes of many of its sympathizers, with the collapse of the Soviet Union and the sister Stalinist regimes in 1989–1991, skepticism and pessimism on the left took hold. Neoliberalism had apparently triumphed. The postmodern/discursive turn in the academy provided intellectual cover for that shift, with its main charge that "classical Marxism" and its "privileging" of the proletariat, especially those in "the West," had outlived its usefulness. Thus, fertile intellectual ground was prepared for what Robinson had to offer, rescuing him from obscurity.[87]

Trying to make a case for the authentic Marx project at that moment proved to be a challenge, and I collected a pile of publishers' rejection letters. "Swimming against the current" is the not-too-subtle message of those from left venues. Luckily, a mainstream academic press, State University of New York, thought otherwise. *Marx and Engels: Their Contribution to the Democratic Breakthrough* saw the light of day in the same year Robinson's faux-Marx project reappeared.

African revolutionary Thomas Sankara is also absent in *Black Marxism* and the 2000 Foreword; specifically, when his significance would have been well known to those who claimed to be Black revolutionaries. What did Sankara have in common with Bishop and Malcolm? All three were embraced in their lifetimes and had their ideas promoted—their speeches and interviews kept in print until today—by a party that calls itself Marxist, and a mostly white one, the Socialist Workers Party. The SWP, in other words, did exactly what Robinson claimed Marxists were incapable of doing. The origins of that embrace go back to that all-important correction Marx made on the Irish question that

Lenin seized on and actively drummed into the heads of a group of American communists who would later found the SWP. Rather than acknowledge and applaud the embrace, as did Malcolm X, Robinson chose silence, thus the exclusion of the three revolutionaries from his text.

Cornel West complains that those who criticize Robinson are being "sectarian to the brotha."[88] But it's Robinson who was the sectarian: the politics of exclusion from his cultural nationalist sect. This is why Douglass, I suspect, was persona non grata in Robinson's church—not even a mention in *Black Marxism*—because the abolitionist never subscribed to race-fundamentalism and race-exclusion political work. But Douglass used his *Monthly* newspaper to teach about Toussaint L'Ouverture, Denmark Vesey, and Nat Turner—which, in theory, should have endeared him to Robinson and his "Black radical tradition."

Black Marxism provides progressive intellectual cover for petit bourgeois cultural entrepreneurs—hence its popularity in those quarters.[89] In denying the revolutionary potential of the proletariat, it enables that social layer's ever-present campaign to mislead the Black masses by posing as the alternative leadership, the cat's-paw for the Democratic Party.

It is inexcusable today, when there is for the first time a real Black bourgeoisie and Black meritocracy, to be silent, as was Robinson, about class divisions within Black America. The African American population, to repeat, is more proletarian than ever, hence, more class-divided than ever, making the possibility of alliances with the proletariat of other identities more likely—why the slogan "Black Lives Matter" is at best inadequate and at worst an obstacle toward that end. Too bad, as someone once savvily suggested, that "when Black lives matter, all lives matter" didn't become the slogan of preference.

The proletarian factor was on telling display in the November

2024 presidential election. The Democratic Party's race card no longer had currency for the Black proletariat as it once did for more than a half-century. Millions voted as workers for the first time, and not as Blacks, owing to so-called pocketbook issues. It testifies to how much more racially integrated the U.S. working class is today—and bodes well for Maurice Bishop's advice to African Americans a half-century ago: that "the Black movement in America" should forge "the firmest and closest links with the white working-class movement."

But what's the road forward to a working-class-led "radical redistribution of economic and political power"? The challenge that those of us who argue for the revolutionary potential of the proletariat is that virtually no one is alive today who witnessed the last time the proletariat was in revolutionary or near-revolutionary mode in an advanced capitalist country, specifically the United States—where humanity's most lethal weapons are housed and thus where its future it likely to be decided. Only if its working class takes power can the world be assured that those weapons will never be employed. The hegemonic epistemology that fetishizes only what we can see to be truth, inevitable in a capitalist society, makes the task of envisioning working-class ascent in the United States even harder. Therein is the indispensability of historical knowledge when it comes to human experience.

What brought that last radicalization in the 1930s to an end? In a nutshell, the Second World War, the combination of wartime patriotism and wartime spending. The former, which undermined class consciousness and thus class struggle was aided and abetted by the latter, which ended the Depression. Followed by Washington's emergence from the conflagration as capital's dominant world power, the U.S. working class achieved upward mobility as never before—the American Dream. That achievement was accompanied by a key political one, the co-optation of the once independently organized militant labor movement into the Democratic Party, a capitalist party, where the movement was housebroken. I'd be derelict to not mention that cancer on the workers' movement, Stalinism. Not only did that faux-communist project enable the Democrat Party's co-optation of the labor movement, the CPUSA's "popular front" policy, but it also soured millions of workers on "Marxism" by being the chief apologist for the horrors done by Moscow and its sycophants in the name of communism.[90]

Only about half, if that, of the U.S. working class today believes in the Dream—this is what MAGA registers, and why the Democratic Party exerts less influence inside the working class than ever.[91] Also, different, and most important, despite liberal angst about the Trump moment, is that the American proletariat is more racially integrated, hence more racially tolerant than it's ever been. The 1930s radicalization took place in the era of Jim Crow and thus was limited in how revolutionary it could be. The respect that the proletarian-based civil rights movement won from white workers everywhere—including in the old Confederacy—goes a long way toward explaining an American proletariat less racist than ever—what the luck of the genes permits this African American octogenarian to verify. Finally, Stalinism, still extant, also exerts less influence than ever in the U.S. workers' movement.

"Inevitable," it can't be said enough, appears only once in the *Communist Manifesto,* followed immediately by instructions for the proletariat about how to take power. The argument here is that conditions have never been better to do so. History teaches what happens when a real working-class radicalization takes place but fails to replace the rule of capital—the tragic prelude to the Second World War; think post–World War One, France, Germany and Spain. German fascism, never to be forgotten, triumphed on the ashes of three failed prior revolutions in that country.[92] In the Trump era, a nuclear-armed world, where capitalist wars are already under way—Putin's war against Ukraine—or threatened, owing to Trump's beggar-thy-neighbor tariffs offensive—the stakes for humanity today could not be higher. Tarriff wars can lead to shooting wars.

With remarkable accuracy, Engels predicted in 1892 that the next European war would claim the lives of "fifteen to twenty million armed men" owing to the increased lethality of weapons then in production.[93] But such a war was not—as he had said presciently in 1888, remarkably also—inevitable if Russia's toilers were able to overthrow their ruling class.[94] Though too late to prevent the "Great War" that commenced in August 1914, the seizure of state power by Russia's workers and peasants in October 1917 did initiate the beginning to the end of the greatest slaughter humanity had ever suffered. This is a rich inheritance, Engels's insight, that this claim draws from about how to prevent a Third World War, one that would most likely spell the end of our species—to wit, working-class ascent.

We can be confident that big class battles lie ahead of us. The ever-deepening crisis of capitalism ensures that sobering fact. The best it has to offer the working class is behind us. The crucial question is whether there will be in place, when that history-making moment arrives, the kind of battle-tested and disciplined leadership, clear on "what is to be done," needed to channel the rightful anger of millions of workers into a constructive outcome in the interests of the world's toilers. We, the subjects of class society, have been resisting our oppression since the dawn of class society ten millennia ago—what the first part of the *Communist Manifesto* distills. Our side, in other words, knows how to express its anger, how to resist. The challenge ever since has been rather about how to take power, to win—what the rest of the *Manifesto* is about.

If a revolutionary workers' party doesn't exist when a revolutionary moment occurs, as Lenin so presciently explained in 1901, it will be "too late to form the organization in times of explosion and outburst."[95] History is strewn with the corpses of would-be revolutions that didn't know about or failed to heed his wisdom—the tragedy of the Arab Spring. The more than century-old question about whether a socialist revolution is possible in the United States increasingly becomes, what happens in a nuclear-armed world if such a revolution doesn't take place? This collection of articles aims to bring clarity to one of the crucial questions for that fateful moment, its arrival that no one can predict—the necessary preparatory work.

CEDRIC ROBINSON CORRECTLY RECOGNIZED that there is indeed a fundamental incompatibility between "Black Marxism" and the real Marxist project and, hence, his rejection of the latter. In contrast to his apolitical and ideational perspective for explaining social reality, Marx's project began with that youthful epiphany in 1844 that "ideas cannot carry out anything at all." For that to happen "men are needed." And Marx's conclusion a year later to part company with the world of philosophy, to make "politics, participation in politics . . . *real struggles*, the starting point of our criticism," a perspective that's alien to *Black Marxism* and exactly why the book ignored the real world of politics when written.[96] As to which "men," Marx, in partnership with Engels, arrived at an answer shortly afterward. For the opponents of Marx's project, like Robinson, if not the proletariat, in all its skin colors, genders, and nationalities, then which layer of society do we look to for "human emancipation"? If you feel no obligation to supply an alternative, please explain why.

For those interested in revolutionary politics, not only currently but also historically, such as the Second American Revolution, *Black Marxism,* to put it bluntly, is not only useless but in today's world, dangerous—a chimera, a faux solution. They'd do better, as did Du Bois, with the actual Marx.

Bibliography

Alagraa, Bedour. "Cedric Robinson's *Black Marxism*: Thirty-Five Years Later," *The CLR James Journal*, Vol. 24, No.1–2 (Fall 2018).

Allen, Robert. *Black Awakening in Capitalist America: An Analytic History* (New York: Doubleday, 1970).

Arnesen, Eric. *Waterfront Workers in New Orleans: Race, Class and Politics, 1863–1923* (Urbana: University of Illinois Press, 1991).

Avineri, Shlomo. *Karl Marx: Philosophy and Revolution* (New Haven: Yale University Press, 2019).

Barnes, James. *Malcolm X: Black Liberation & the Road to Workers Power* (New York: Pathfinder Press, 2009).

Blassingame, John, ed. *The Frederick Douglass Papers: Series One: Speeches, Debates and Interviews, Volumes 1, 2, 3: 1855–63* (New Haven: Yale University Press, 1979–1985).

Blight, David. *Frederick Douglass: Prophet of Freedom* (New York: Simon & Schuster, 2018).

Breitman, George, ed. *Leon Trotsky on Black Nationalism and Self-Determination* (New York: Pathfinder Press, 1972).

Cannon, James P. *The First Ten Years of American Communism: Report of a Participant* (New York: Lyle Stuart, 1962).

Carew, Jan. *Ghosts in Our Blood: With Malcolm X in Africa, England, and the Caribbean* (Chicago: Lawrence Hill Books, 1994).

Clark, Steve. "The Second Assassination of Maurice Bishop," *New International*, No. 6 (1987).

Collins, Henry, and Chimen Abramsky. *Karl Marx and the British Labour Movement: Years of the First International* (London: Macmillan, 1965).

Cox, Oliver. *Caste, Class, and Race* (New York: Modern Reader, 1970).

Douglas, Andrew J., and Jared A. Loggins. *Prophet of Discontent: Martin Luther King Jr. and the Critique of Racial Capitalism* (Athens: University of Georgia Press, 2021).

Draper, Hal. *The Annotated Communist Manifesto* (Berkeley, CA: Center for Social History, 1984).

Draper, Hal. "Marx and the Economic-Jew Stereotype," from *Karl Marx's Theory of Revolution, vol. 1: State and Bureaucracy* (New York: Monthly Review Press, 1977).

Dreier, Peter. "A True and Visionary Radical, Martin Luther King, Jr. Was No Moderate," *Countercurrents.org*, January 17, 2023, https://countercurrents.org/2023/01/a-true-and-visionary-radical-martin-luther-king-jr-was-no-moderate/.

Du Bois, W. E. B. *Black Reconstruction in America, 1860–1880: Introduction by David Levering Lewis* (New York: Free Press, 1998).

Du Bois, W. E. B. "Karl Marx and the Negro," in A. Zimmerman, ed., *The Civil War in the United States: Karl Marx and Frederick Engels* (New York: International Publishers, 2016).

Edwards, Kyle. " 'Those Deluded, Ill-Starred Men': Frederick Douglass, the New National Era, and the Paris Commune," *New North Star*, Vol. 4, No. 1 (December 19, 2022), https://doi.org/10.18060/26926.

Eig, Jonathan. *King: A Life* (New York: Farrar, Straus and Giroux, 2023).

Enmale, Richard, ed. *Karl Marx and Friedrich Engels: The Civil War in the United States* (New York: International Publishers, 1937).

Fairclough, Adam. *Race & Democracy: The Civil Rights Struggle in Louisiana, 1915–1972* (Athens: University of *Georgia* Press, 1995).

Ferguson, Thomas, et al. "The Roots of Right-Wing Populism: Donald Trump in 2016," *International Journal of Political Economy*, Vol. 49, No. 2 (2020).

Foner, Eric. *Reconstruction: America's Unfinished Revolution, 1863–1877* (New York: Harper & Row, 1988).

Foster, John Bellamy, Hannah Hollerman, and Brett Clark. "Marx and Slavery," *Monthly Review*, Vol. 72, No. 3 (July/August 2020).

George, Charles H. *500 Years of Revolution: European Radicals from Hus to Lenin* (Chicago: Charles H. Kerr, 1998).

Geuss, Raymond. *Philosophy and Real Politics* (Princeton, NJ: Princeton University Press, 2008).

Geuss, Raymond."The Moral Legacy of Marxism," *Analyse & Kritik*, Vol. 3, No. 1–2 (2015).

Grim, Ryan. "The Elephant in the Zoom," *The Intercept*, June 13, 2022, https://theintercept.com/2022/06/13/progressive-organizing-infighting-callout-culture/.

Hannah-Jones, Nikole, Caitlin Roper, Ilena Silverman, Jake Silverstein, eds. *The 1619 Project* (New York: One World, 2021).

Haverty-Stacke, Donna T., *Trotskyists on Trial: Free Speech and Political Persecution Since the Age of FDR* (New York: New York University Press, 2008).

Hund, Wulf. "Marx and Haiti: Note on a Blank Space," *Journal of World Philosophies*, Vol. 6, No. 2 (January 2021), https://scholarworks.iu.edu/iupjournals/index.php/jwp/article/view/4918/358.

James, C.L.R. *Trotskyism in the United States, 1940-1947: The Workers Party and the Johnson Forest Tendency*, https://www.marxists.org/archive/james-clr/works/1947/balance-sheet/index.htm

Johnson, Cedric. "The Wrong Durée: The Politics of Cedric J. Robinson's Racial Capitalism," *Nonsite.org*, January 29, 2025, https://nonsite.org/the-wrong-duree-the-politics-of-cedric-j-robinsons-racial-capitalism/.

Joseph, Peniel E. *The Sword and the Shield: The Revolutionary Lives of Malcolm X and Martin Luther King Jr.* (New York: Basic Books, 2020).

Kelley, Robin D. G. "Foreword," *Black Marxism: The Making of the Black Radical Tradition*, by Cedric Robinson (Chapel Hill, NC: University of North Carolina Press, 2000).

Kelley, Robin D. G. "What Did Cedric Robinson Mean by Racial Capitalism?" *Boston Review*, January 12, 2017, https://www.bostonreview.net/articles/robin-d-g-kelley-introduction-race-capitalism-justice/.

Kelly, Brian. "Slave Self-Activity and the Bourgeois Revolution in the United States: Jubilee and the Boundaries of Black Freedom," *Historical Materialism*, Vol. 27, No. 3 (2019).

Kelly, Joseph. "Organized for a Fair Deal: African American Railway Workers in the Deep South, 1900–1940" (Ph.D. Diss., University of Toronto, 2010).

Krader, Lawrence. *The Ethnological Notebooks of Karl Marx* (Assen, The Netherlands: Van Gorcum, 1972).

Leon, Abram. *The Jewish Question: A Marxist Interpretation* (Atlanta, GA: Pathfinder Press, 2020).

Levine, Bruce. *The Fall of the House of Dixie: The Civil War and the Social Revolution that Transformed the South* (New York: Random House, 2013).

Liedman, Sven-Eric. *A World to Win: The Life and Work of Karl Marx* (London: Verso, 2018).

Lowery, Wesley. *America's Backlash: A Changing Nation and the Cost of Progress* (New York: HarperCollins, 2023).

McNally, David. "It's Called Capitalism: Naming the System Behind Systemic Racism: An Interview with Keeanga-Yamahtta Taylor," *Spectre Journal,* June 1, 2022, https://spectrejournal.com/its-called-capitalism-naming-the-system-behind-systemic-racism.

Mandel, Ernest. *The Second Slump: A Marxist Analysis of Recession in the Seventies* (London: New Left Books, 1978).

Mandela, Nelson, and Fidel Castro. *How Far We Slaves Have Come! South Africa and Cuba in Today's World* (New York: Pathfinder Press, 1991).

Marcus, Bruce, and Mike Taber, eds. *Maurice Bishop Speaks: The Grenada Revolution, 1979–83* (New York: Pathfinder Press, 1983).

Martin, Tony. "C. L. R. James and the Race/Class Question," *Race,* Vol. 14, No. 2, (1972), https://doi.org/10.1177/030639687201400204.

Marx, Karl. *Capital,* Vol. 1, (New York: International Publishers, 1972).

Marx, Karl. *Capital,* Vol. 1, "Appendix: Results of the Immediate Process of Production" (New York: Penguin Books, 1976).

Marx, Karl, and Friedrich Engels. *Collected Works* (New York: International Publishers, 1975–2004).

Nimtz, August H. *Islam and Politics in East Africa,* (Minneapolis: University of Minnesota Press, 1980).

Nimtz, August H. "Marxism and the Black Struggle: A Review Article," *Journal of African Marxists* (London: Journal of African Marxists, 1985).

Nimtz, August H. *Marx and Engels: Their Contribution to the Democratic Breakthrough* (Albany, NY: SUNY Press, 2000).

Nimtz, August H. "The Eurocentric Marx and Engels and Other Related Myths," *Marxism, Modernity and Postcolonial Studies,* ed. Crystal Bartolovich and Neil Lazarus (New York: Cambridge University Press, 2002).

Nimtz, August H. *Marx, Tocqueville, and Race in America: The "Absolute Democracy" or "Defiled Republic"* (Lanham, MD: Lexington Books, 2003).

Nimtz, August H. "Natural versus Social Phenomena: Cuba and the Lessons of Katrina," *Black Scholar,* Vol. 36, No. 4 (Winter 2006).

Nimtz, August H. *Lenin's Electoral Strategy from Marx and Engels Through the Revolution of 1905: The Ballot, the Streets—Or Both* (New York: Palgrave Macmillan, 2014).

Nimtz, August H., *Lenin's Electoral Strategy from 1907 to the October Revolution of 1917: The Ballot, the Streets—or Both* (New York: Palgrave Macmillan, 2014).

Nimtz, August H. "A Black Socialist in Trump Country," *Minneapolis Star Tribune*, July 29, 2016, https://www.startribune.com/a-black-socialist-in-trump-country/388716201.

Nimtz, August H. "The Graveyard of Progressive Social Movements: The Black Hole of the Democratic Party," *MR Online*, May 9, 2017, https://mronline.org/2017/05/09/the-graveyard-of-progressive-social-movements/.

Nimtz, August H. "The Meritocratic Myopia of Ta-Nehisi Coates," *MR Online*, November 17, 2017, https://mronline.org/2017/11/17/the-meritocratic-myopia-of-ta-nehisi-coates/.

Nimtz, August H. "History and Contingency in the Making of a Black Communist," *Minneapolis Interview Project*, 2018–2020, https://turtleroad.org/2019/10/11/august-nimtz-geography-of-a-black-communist/.

Nimtz, August H. *Marxism versus Liberalism: Comparative Real-Time Political Analysis* (New York: Palgrave Macmillan, 2019).

Nimtz, August H. "Bernie Sanders and the 'Two Diseases of Bourgeois Politics': 'Parliamentary Cretinism' and 'Voting Fetishism,'" *Science & Society* [forthcoming].

Nimtz, August H., and Kyle A. Edwards, *The Communist and the Revolutionary Liberal in the Second American Revolution: Comparing Karl Marx and Frederick Douglass in Real Time* (Chicago: Haymarket Press, 2025).

Novack, George. *America's Revolutionary Heritage* (Atlanta, GA: Pathfinder Press, 2013).

Oakes, James. *Freedom National: The Destruction of Slavery in the United States: 1861–1865* (New York: W. W. Norton, 2013).

Ralph, Michael, and Maya Singhal. "Racial Capitalism," *Theory and Society*, Vol. 48 (December 20, 2019).

Reed, Adolph, Jr. "Du Bois and the 'Wages of Whiteness': What He Meant, What He Didn't, and, Besides, It Shouldn't Matter for Our Politics Anyway," *Nonsite.org*, June 29, 2017, https://nonsite.org/du-bois-and-the-wages-of-whiteness/.

Reynolds, David S. *John Brown, Abolitionist: The Man Who Killed Slavery, Sparked the Civil War, and Seeded Civil Rights* (New York: Alfred Knopf, 2005).

Riazanov, David. *Karl Marx and Frederick Engels* (New York: Monthly Review Press, 1973).

Richardson, Heather Cox. *Death of Reconstruction: Race, Labor, and Politics in the Post–Civil War North, 1865–1901* (Cambridge, MA: Harvard University Press, 2001).

Riddell, John, ed. *Workers of the World and Oppressed Peoples, Unite! Proceedings and Documents of the Second Congress, 1920, Vol. One* (New York: Pathfinder Press, 1991).

Roberts, Michael. *The Long Depression: How It Happened, Why It Happened, and What Happens Next* (Chicago: Haymarket Books, 2016).

Robinson, Cedric J. *Black Marxism: The Making of the Black Radical Tradition* (London: Zed Books, 1983; Chapel Hill, NC: University of North Carolina Press, 2000).

Robinson, William I., Salvador Rangel, and Hilbourne A. Watson "The Cult of Cedric Robinson's *Black Marxism*: A Proletarian Critique," *Midwestern Marx Institute,* October 3, 2022, https://www.midwesternmarx.com/articles/the-cult-of-cedric-robinsons-black-marxism-a-proletarian-critique-by-william-i-robinson-salvador-rangel-and-hilbourne-a-watson.

Robinson, William I., Salvador Rangel, and Hilbourne A. Watson. "A Proletarian Critique of Cedric Robinson's Black Marxism, Take 2," *The Philosophical Salon,* June 30, 2025, https://thephilosophicalsalon.com/a-proletarian-critique-of-cedric-robinsons-black-marxism-take-2/.

Rogers, Kim Lacy. *Righteous Lives: Narratives of the New Orleans Civil Rights Movement* (New York: New York University Press, 1993).

Rowan, Steven, and James Primm. *Germans for a Free Missouri* (Columbia: University of Missouri Press, 1983).

Said, Edward. *Orientalism* (New York: Vintage, 1979).

Sinha, Manisha. *The Slave's Cause: A History of Abolition* (New Haven: Yale University Press, 2016).

Slack, Gregory. "Did Marx Defend Black Slavery? On Jamaica and Labour in Black Skin," *Historical Materialism,* Vol. 31, No. 2 & 3 (April 2023), https://www.historicalmaterialism.org/article/did-marx-defend-black-slavery/.

Sorentino, Sara-Maria. "The Abstract Slave: Anti-Blackness and Marx's Method," *International Labor and Working-Class History,* No. 96 (Fall 2019).

Sperber, Jonathan. *Karl Marx: A Nineteenth Century Life* (New York: W. W. Norton, 2013).

Stedman-Jones, Gareth. *Karl Marx: Greatness and Illusion* (Cambridge, MA: Harvard University Press, 2013).

Taylor, Kikki M. *America's First Black Socialist: The Radical Life of Peter H. Clark* (Lexington: University of Kentucky Press, 2013).

Trotsky, Leon. *The Revolution Betrayed: What Is the Soviet Union and Where Is It Going?* (New York: Pathfinder Press, 1972).

Trotsky, Leon. *Writings of Leon Trotsky, 1938–39* (New York: Pathfinder Press, 1974).

Vogel, Jeffrey. "The Tragedy of History," *New Left Review*, No. 220 (November/December 1996).

West, Cornel. "Black Radicalism and the Marxist Tradition," *Monthly Review*, Vol. 40, No. 4 (September 1988), https://doi.org/10.14452/MR-040-04-1988-08_5.

Whitaker, Mark. *Saying It Loud: 1966—The Year Black Power Challenged the Civil Rights Movement* (New York: Simon & Schuster, 2023).

Zimmerman, A. "From the Second American Revolution to the First International and Back Again: Marxism, the Popular Front, and the American Civil War," from *The World the Civil War Made*, ed. Gregory Down and Kate Masur (Chapel Hill, NC: University of North Carolina Press, 2015).

Zimmerman, A., ed. "Introduction," *Karl Marx and Friedrich Engels: The Civil War in the United States* (New York: International Publishers, 2016).

Notes

1. Cornel West, "Black Marxism: The Making of the Black Radical Tradition," *Monthly Review,* Vol. 40, no. 4 (September 1988): 51, https://doi.org/10.14452/MR-040-04-1988-08_5.
2. August H. Nimtz, Jr., "Review: Marxism and the Black Struggle: The 'Class v. Race' Debate Revisited," *Journal of African Marxists/Journal des marxistes africains* [London], vol. 7 (1985): 75–89.
3. Robin D. G. Kelley, Foreword to *Black Marxism: The Making of the Black Radical Tradition* by Cedric Robinson, 2nd ed. (Chapel Hill, NC: University of North Carolina Press, 2000), xviii.
4. Mario Soares Neto, "Black Marxism?" *a terra é redonda,* March 11, 2021, https://en.aterraeredonda.com.br/marxismo-negro/ (About the limits of Google Scholar see the end of this Preface.)
5. Kelley, Foreword to *Black Marxism,* xxvii.
6. Soares Neto, in *Academia.* The site likely generated recognition of the review, in chronological order, in these publications: https://thephilosophicalsalon.com/the-cult-of-cedric-robinsons-black-marxism-a-proletarian-critique/; https://nonsite.org/the-wrong-duree-the-politics-of-cedric-j-robinsons-racial-capitalism/; https://jacobin.com/2025/02/black-marxists-du-bois-king.
7. August H. Nimtz, "Black Marxism and Black Socialism with Professor August H. Nimtz," *YouTube,* May 17, 2021, https://www.youtube.com/watch?v=bklxXZ5uNR0.
8. Respectively, *Marx and Engels: Their Contribution to the Democratic Breakthrough* (Albany, NY: SUNY Press, 2000); *Marx, Tocqueville, and Race*

in America: The 'Absolute Democracy' or 'Defiled Republic' (Lanham, MD: Lexington Books, 2003); *Marxism versus Liberalism: Comparative Real-Time Political Analysis* (New York: Palgrave-Macmillan, 2019); coauthored with Kyle A. Edwards, *The Communist and the Revolutionary Liberal in the Second American Revolution: Comparing Karl Marx and Frederick Douglass in Real-Time* (Boston: Brill, 2024).

9. See Kelley, Foreword to *Black Marxism*, xix-xxvi.
10. Nimtz and Edwards, *The Communist and the Revolutionary Liberal in the Second American Revolution* (Leiden, The Netherlands: Brill, 2024).
11. Admittedly, I'm taking liberties here with Robinson's "Black radical tradition" concept because Frederick Douglass doesn't even rate a mention in his narrative—which raises questions about its utility.
12. Kelley, Foreword to *Black Marxism*, xi.
13. Another deserved presence but absent in his narrative: John Brown. See chapter 5.
14. Kelley, Foreword to *Black Marxism*, xix.
15. Ibid., xv.
16. "I was more interested in becoming a full-time Communist than a full-time scholar." Ibid., xi.
17. Robinson, *Black Marxism*, p. 402n187.

1. Fortuitous Biography as Prelude

1. Karl Marx, *The Eighteenth Brumaire of Louis Bonaparte.* Karl Marx and Friedrich Engels, *Collected Works* (New York: International Publishers, 1975-2004, Vol. 11, 103.
2. Historian Rien Fertel provides a useful introductory overview. Rien Fertel, "Confederate Monuments and Labor Integration in New Orleans," Lectures in History, New Orleans, C-Span, March 20, 2024, https://www.c-span.org/video/?533987-1/confederate-monuments-labor-integration-orleans.
3. August H. Nimtz, "August Nimtz: History and Contingency in the Making of a Black Communist," Interview by Anne Winkler-Morey, *Minneapolis Interview Project*, October 11, 2019, https://turtleroad.org/2019/10/11/august-nimtz-geography-of-a-black-communist/. I'm forever indebted to Anne Winkler-Morey who invited me to do a political autobiographical interview in 2018. Ongoing research on the founders of modern communism at the time taught that, if you don't tell your own story, others will, and in ways you might disagree with.
4. For some useful history of the local, see *Historypin*, https://www.historypin.org/en/explore/geo/37.77493,-122.419416,12/bounds/37.712353,-122.488767,37.837454,-122.350065/paging/1/pin/ 1154301.
5. Adam Fairclough, *Race & Democracy: The Civil Rights Struggle in Louisiana, 1915–1972* (Athens: University of Georgia Press, 1995), 211.

6. About the school and Mr. Spriggins, see "History of the Normal School at McDonogh # 35 and Valena C. Jones," *Creolegen*, October 29, 2015, https://www.creolegen.org/2015/10/29/history-of-the-normal-school-at-mcdonogh-35-and-valena-c-jones-1923-1939/.
7. Fairclough, *Race and Democracy*, 202–3.
8. Richard Sandomir, "Jack O'Dell, King Aide Fired Over Communist Past, Dies at 96," *New York Times*, November 19, 2019, https://www.nytimes.com/2019/11/19/us/jack-odell-dead.html.
9. About the state's effort to seize NAACP membership lists and records, and the counter effort, see Fairclough, *Race and Democracy*, 196–97.
10. Ibid., 162–63. Also, Kim Lacy Rogers, *Righteous Lives: Narratives of the New Orleans Civil Rights Movement* (New York: New York University Press, 1993), 38–40.
11. Rogers, *Righteous Lives*, 41–44.
12. Ibid., 43. Sadly, Rogers, a 1983 University of Minnesota history PhD, is no longer alive for me to thank her for this invaluable find. Dr. Mack J. Spears, the principal of McDonogh 35, and close colleague of my mother, I later learned, recruited me to attend the school. He was on a mission to raise its academic standards. Only later did I realize that I had received special attention, such as that afforded by Mr. Spriggins. I graduated in 1959 as salutatorian; my girlfriend, Jocelyn Chatters, after transferring to 35 from Xavier Prep to complete her senior year—the private school fees for continuing there proved to be prohibitive for her family—graduated as valedictorian. I have, alas, no memories of how I first found my way to the main public library. Speculating on the significance of the special treatment I received merits another essay that, hopefully, I can one day write.
13. That moment is when the White Citizens Council initiated a campaign against the NAACP to purge Blacks from voter rolls—the counter-offensive against the 1954 SCOTUS decision. See Fairclough, *Race and Democracy*, chapter 8.
14. Joseph Kelly, "Organized for a Fair Deal: African American Railway Workers in the Deep South, 1900–1940" (PhD diss., University of Toronto, 2010), 122n71.
15. Because my father objected to being drafted into a segregated army to serve in the Second World War, he was allowed, as a substitute, to work at the Naval Ammunition Depot in Hawthorne, NV. His younger brother, Melvin, however, did serve in a segregated Marines unit in the Pacific theater.
16. Revius Ortique, Jr., the union's lawyer, played a key role in the city's civil rights movement. See Fairclough, *Race and Democracy*, Index.
17. New Orleans historian Eric Arnesen argues in *Waterfront Workers of New Orleans: Race, Class, and Politics, 1863–1923* (Champaign: University of Illinois Press,1991), that New Orleans was unique in the South for interracial

union organizing, particularly on the waterfront. Given its proximity to the Custom House where my father worked, it's possible that he was aware of that history. I'll never forget him being totally absorbed in a copy of Arnesen's book that he found on his own in my library during a visit in the mid-1990s.

18. About that world, in which new Pope Leo XIV has roots, see Richard Fausset and Robert Chiarito, "New Pope Has Creole Roots in New Orleans," *New York Times,* May 8, 2025, https://www.nytimes.com/2025/05/08/us/pope-leo-creole-new-orleans.html. Also, Campbell Roberson, "Pope's Family History Offers a Glimpse Into the American Creole Journey," *New York Times,* May 11, 2025, https://www.nytimes.com/2025/05/11/us/creole-identity-history-pope-new-orleans.html.
19. See https://www.asanet.org/e-franklin-frazier/. Also, https://www.simonandschuster.com/books/Black-Bourgeoisie/Franklin-Frazier/9780684832418.
20. For example, Malcolm mentions "Franklin Frazier in his book *The Black Bourgeoisie* . . . and I would advise you, read this book . . . get it . . . [to know] the difference between the house Negro and the field Negro [April 16, 1961]." *Malcolm X, Collected Speeches, Debates & Interviews,* Vol. 1 *(1960-1963),* ed. Sandeep S. Atwal (Toronto: Any Means Necessary, 2018), 48–49.
21. About the conference, the program, and a later assessment, see "PROGRAM: National Conference on South African Crisis and American Action, March 21–23, 1965, https://africanactivist.msu.edu/recordFiles/210-849-20634/1965confprogram.pdf; and "1965 Report: January 31, 1965 through December 31, 1965," https://africanactivist.msu.edu/recordFiles/210-849-30108/PWACOAAR65opt.pdf.
22. Mark Whitaker, *Saying It Loud: 1966—The Year Black Power Challenged the Civil Rights Movement* (New York: Simon & Schuster, 2023).
23. For an assessment of what that course implied, see Jack Barnes, *Malcolm X: Black Liberation & the Road to Workers Power* (Atlanta, GA: Pathfinder Press, 2010), Part 4.
24. The dissertation became, in 1980, *Islam and Politics in East Africa: The Sufi Order in Tanzania* (Minneapolis: University of Minnesota Press, 1980).
25. For details, see Robin D. G. Kelley, foreword to *Black Marxism: The Making of the Black Radical Tradition* by Cedric Robinson, 2nd ed. (Chapel Hill: University of North Carolina Press, 2000), xxii–xiv.
26. On the academic background to that decision, see "August Nimtz: History and Contingency in the Making of a Black Communist," by Anne Winkler-Morey, https://turtleroad.org/2019/10/11/august-nimtz-geography-of-a-black-communist/. Earlier that year I interviewed at Howard University. But to get a job there I had to sign a document saying that I wasn't a member of "the Communist Party"—one of the reasons I declined the offer when it later arrived.
27. See October 27, 2018, in "Affirmative Action: Curse or Cure?" my letter to

the *New York Times* in which I rejected columnist Bret Stephens's presumption that I should be forever damaged for having been told what the chair said about my hire, https://www.nytimes.com/2018/10/27/opinion/letters/affirmative-action.html.

28. About the NSM, see "Northern Student Movement," *Digital SNCC Gateway*, https://sncedigital.org/inside-sncc/alliances-relationships/northern-student -movement/.
29. As Malcolm explained in February 1965: "Up until the time of the [Second World] war, you couldn't get inside of a plant. I lived in Lansing, where Oldsmobile's factory was, and Reo's. There was about three in the whole plant and each one of them had a broom. They had education. They had gone to school. I think one had gone to college. But he was a 'broomologist.'" Malcolm X, "Malcolm X on Not Just an American Problem, but a World Problem (Feb. 16, 1965)," *ICIT Digital Library*, https://www.icit-digital.org/articles/malcolm-x-on-not-just-an-american-problem-but-a-world-problem-feb-16-1965. Malcolm, in other words, could have been describing my reality at that moment, had I remained in the plant.
30. For details, see Donna T. Haverty-Stacke, *Trotskyists on Trial: Free Speech and Political Persecution since the Age of FDR* (New York: New York University Press, 2008), index entries. I'll never forget once being on a *Militant* sales team with Harry five years later, a privilege I now recognize. A meeting to organize ourselves, before the three-hour drive to the Iron Range where a strike was underway, required comrades to be there early that morning. Harry arrived before anyone—a standard I learned, if not always living up to it.
31. See "August Nimtz: History and Contingency in the Making of a Black Communist," by Anne Winkler-Morey, *Minneapolis Interview Project*, for details about my party years, https://turtleroad.org/2019/10/11/august-nimtz-geography -of-a-black-communist/.
32. My writings for *The Militant*, between 1979 and 1980, and occasionally in other years, are now available online, owing to the volunteer Pathfinder Print Project: https://themilitant.com/?s=.
33. "Negros to Study Foreign Affairs; Capital Institute to Prepare 40 to Serve in Agencies," *New York Times*, May 17, 1964, https://www.nytimes.com/1964/05/17/archives/negroes-to-study-foreign-affairs-capital-institute-to-prepare-40-to.html.
34. In addition to Monk, the rest of the quartet consisted of Charlie Rouse on tenor sax, Ben Riley on drums, and Butch Warren on bass. I confess that I was a bit disappointed that Rouse, and not Johnny Griffin, would be the saxophonist. Not disappointed enough, though, to keep me away the next three nights. Unforgettable were the moments when Monk, in his own world, wandered away from the piano between solos, and the uncertainty, at least

for me, whether he would return in time to finish a piece. The income tax refund that made the experience possible derived from my one-year as sommelier at Harvey's Famous Restaurant on Connecticut Avenue, a job that I faked my way into in September 1963. Also indelibly printed on my memory banks were the sublime flavors of a half bottle of 1959 Chateau Margaux that I sneaked away one night. Too bad I didn't know enough then about how to truly savor it.

2. *Black Marxism*: The First In-Depth Review

1. Cuba's then ambassador to Tanzania, Armando Entralgo, as he explained to me in a conversation in Havana in 1991, evidently played a major role in that defeat. Because of his government's exemplary record of defending African self-determination (the best was yet to come), U.S. cultural nationalists met opposition that he helped organize to their insistence that skin color determine revolutionary bona fides. Entralgo—with the approval of Tanzanian authorities, he told me—ensured that such criteria would not find their way into the conference's final documents, to the disappointment of the nationalists.
2. In the most complete archives about that work in the United States, there is only one, maybe, reference to "Cedric Robinson." See https://africanactivist.msu.edu/.
3. See, for example, August H. Nimtz, *Marx, Tocqueville, and Race in America* (Lanham, MD: Lexington Books, 2003), 206–207.
4. Another Cedric, Cedric Johnson, is to be applauded for being the exception to today's scholars by exposing the theoretical, as well as political, deficits in Robinson's tome. See his "Wrong Durée: The Politics of Cedric J. Robinson's Racial Capitalism," *Nonsite.org*, January 29, 2025, *https://nonsite.org/the-wrong-duree-the-politics-of-cedric-j-robinsons-racial-capitalism/*.
5. I elaborate on the point in my revisit to *Black Marxism* in chapter 5.
6. About *JAM*'s origins and end, see David Seddon's article on the Roape website and journal, "'For the Labouring People,'" *Review of African Political Economy*, July 5, 2018, https://roape.net/2018/07/05/for-the-labouring-people/. Thanks to Jean Allman and David Roediger for sharing.
7. My article, "The Making and Unmaking of a Revolution: Some Lessons from Grenada," was published in the Dar es Salaam-based journal *The African Review*, Vol. 12, No. 2 (1985).
8. See the informative eulogy in the *African Journal of Political Economy*, https://d.lib.msu.edu/ajpe/32.
9. Robert Allen, *Black Awakening in Capitalist America: An Analytic History*, (New York: Doubleday, 1970), 265.
10. This review understandably cannot take up the many aspects of Robinson's argument. One of these is his claim that Blacks fared well under Islam and

Arab rule (116–25). My own research, see, for instance, *Islam and Politics in East Africa* (Minneapolis: University of Minnesota Press, 1980), suggests that Blacks in the Arab-Muslim world encountered, if not similar problems as those in a Christian European context, certainly racist ones. European imperialism also played a role.

11. Cedric Robinson, *Black Marxism: The Making of the Black Radical Tradition* (London: Zed Books, 1983; Chapel Hill, N.C.: University of North Carolina Press, 2000), 5.
12. I heard James reaffirm his Marxist credentials in a public lecture at Macalester College, St. Paul, Minnesota, 1976. See also, Tony Martin, "C.L.R. James and the Race/Class Question," *Race*, Vol. 14, No. 2, (1972),:183–93.
13. Engels to Bloch, Sept. 21(22), 1890, Karl Marx and Friedrich Engels, *Selected Correspondence 1844–1895* (Moscow: Progress Publishers, 1975), 395. [Karl Marx and Fredrich Engels, *Collected Works* (New York: International Publishers, 1975-2004, Vol. 49, p. 36; hereafter MECW, 49: 36].
14. Robinson, *Black Marxism*, 53.
15. Robinson, 9.
16. See Ernest Mandel, *The Second Slump: A Marxist Analysis of Recession in the Seventies* (London: New Left Books, 1978).
17. Marx to Weydemeyer, March 5, 1852, *Selected Correspondence*, 64. [MECW, 39: 62-65.]
18. Walter Rodney, *How Europe Underdeveloped Africa* ((Washington, DC: Howard University Press, 1974).
19. A. M. Babu, *African Socialism or Socialist Africa?* (London: Zed Books, 1981).
20. Robinson, 12.
21. Robinson, 211–12.
22. See Marx, *Capital*, Vol. *I* (London: Penguin Books, 1976), 1033–34. The title of this section is "Appendix—Results of the Immediate Process of Production."
23. Marx, *Capital*, Vol. I, 799.
24. Marx to Meyer and Vogt, April 9, 1870, *Selected Correspondence*, 222. [MECW, 43: 474-75.]
25. Marx to Meyer and Vogt, 223. [MECW, 43: 475.]
26. Marx to Engels, December 10, 1869, *Selected Correspondence*, 218. [MECW, 43: 398.] Robinson only quotes the fourth sentence (50) of this and thus denies his readers the opportunity to see how Marx and Engels acknowledged errors.
27. Engels, "The Communists and Karl Heinzen" (1847). [MECW, 6: 303.]
28. If Robinson is referring only to Latin America, his criticism might have some merit since Marx and Engels had almost nothing to say about the independence movement there. It is not clear why. Possibly they had little information about this development.

29. Although he fails to do so, Robinson could have referred to the case of Algeria in making his critique. It is true in an 1848 article Engels opposed the struggle of Abel al-Qadir against French imperialism, saying that the "conquest of Algeria is an important and fortunate fact for the progress of civilization." (Marx and Engels, *Collected Works*, Vol. 6, 471). But Robinson would have been obligated to admit that nine years later Engels reversed himself. Calling the French occupation of Algeria "barbarous," he wrote that the "natives . . . found no advantage in the so-called civilisation of the new government." (Marx and Engels, *On Colonialism*, Moscow: Progress Publishers, 1974, 159.)
30. Marx, "Revolution in China and Europe," May 1853, Marx and Engels, *Collected Works, 1853–54*, Vol.12, 98.
31. Marx and Engels, *On the United States* (Moscow: Progress Publishers, 1979), 73.
32. Marx and Engels, *On the United States, passim.* See also their comments on slave revolts in Jamaica (*On Colonialism*, 322).
33. See Steven Rowan and James Primm, *Germans for a Free Missouri* (Columbia, MO: University of Missouri Press, 1983).
34. See V. I. Lenin, *The National Liberation Movement in the East* (Moscow: Progress Publishers, 1969), *passim.*
35. Part of the problem concerns the categories Du Bois employs in analyzing the post–Civil War Reconstruction period radical governments. He implies that these governments were similar to the workers' governments established in the USSR after the 1917 revolution. If one accepts this questionable thesis—which Robinson does—then indeed it does appear that bourgeois rule was irrelevant to the revolutionary process.
36. Marx and Engels, *On the United States*, 211.
37. David Riazanov, *Karl Marx and Frederick Engels* (New York: Monthly Review, 1973), 100. Also, contrary to Robinson, Lenin learned from them the importance of the peasant question, which was also key in the Bolsheviks' success. See Engels, "The Peasant Question in France and Germany," Karl Marx and Frederick Engels, *Selected Works* (Moscow: Progress Publishers, 1970), 623–40.
38. Robinson, 244.
39. Robinson, 443.
40. Johnson-Forest Tendency, *Balance Sheet: Trotskyism in the United States, 1940-–1947*, August 1947, 12. I am grateful to Fred Feldman, former national education director for the Socialist Workers Party, for making this document available. https://www.marxists.org/archive/james-clr/works/1947/balance-sheet/index.htm.
41. George Breitman (ed.), *Leon Trotsky on Black Nationalism and Self-Determination* (New York: Pathfinder Press, 1972), 25–32. Robinson

acknowledges in a footnote (p.413) that *he* is aware of these discussions but evidently does not think they are significant to mention in the body of his text. See also Tony Martin.

42. Breitman, *Leon Trotsky,* 17–18.
43. See for example the tour of Alejandro Molina Lara, revolutionary trade union leader, from El Salvador in the United States in various issues of *The Militant,* January through March, 1983, https://themilitant.com/back-issue/1983/.
44. Bruce Marcus and Mike Taber (eds.), *Maurice Bishop Speaks: The Grenada Revolution, 1979–83* (New York: Pathfinder Press, 1983), II, 9.

3. The Eurocentric Marx and Engels and Other Related Myths

1. *Marxism, Modernity, and Postcolonial Studies,* ed. Crystal Bartolovich and Neil Lazarus (New York: Cambridge University Press, 2002), 65–80.
2. Karl Marx and Friedrich Engels, *Collected Works* (New York: International Publishers, 1975–2004), Vol. 40, 347; hereafter MECW.
3. MECW, 5:49.
4. MECW, 6:351–52. Though the specifics of Engels's exposition refers only to "civilised countries," that "America" is one of them makes clear that even at this stage their perspective went beyond the European arena.
5. Marx's notebooks indicate that a year earlier he had been reading intensively about British imperialism in Africa and elsewhere in what is currently called the third world. See Marx-Engels 1975b: IV Bd. 6, Text.*Marx-Engels Gesamtausgabe* (MEGA), Berlin: Dietz.
6. MECW, 10:265–66.
7. In a subsequent issue of their *Neue Rheinische Zeitung Revue,* Marx and Engels wrote: "We have already pointed out, before any other European periodical, the importance of the discovery and the consequences it is bound to have for the whole world trade." MECW, 10504.
8. MECW, 10:267.
9. The oft-quoted comment in the *Manifesto* about the "idiocy" of the peasantry and the famous likening of peasants to a "sack of potatoes" have been extensively cited in this respect. Concerning the former, Hal Draper, in *The Annotated Communist Manifesto* (Alameda, CA: Center for Socialist History, 1984), 110–11, has argued convincingly that what is at issue is primarily a matter of mistranslation: it would have been more accurate to have translated "idiocy" as "isolation." As for the latter, it is mainly a problem of taking Marx's words out of context and failing to read further what he had to say; see MECW, 11:187–89.
10. August H. Nimtz, *Marx and Engels: Their Contribution to the Democratic Breakthrough* (Albany, NY: SUNY Press, 2000), see index for entries on the peasantry.
11. MECW, 6:471.

12. MECW, 18:67-69.
13. MECW, 46:242. Though his visit was only for recuperative purposes, it's instructive to note that Marx couldn't help but take an interest in learning about "communal ownership among the Arabs"(MECW, 46:210–11). Lastly, about a half year before his death, Marx reported favorably on anti-imperialist activities in France against British moves in Egypt (MECW, 46:298).
14. MECW, 12:132.
15. MECW, 40:249. Edward Said's failure to acknowledge this side of Marx's views of India, that is, his unequivocal solidarity with Indians who struggled against British rule, leads him to treat Marx erroneously as a nineteenth-century Orientalist. Edward Said, *Orientalism* (New York: Vintage, 1979), 153–57.
16. *The General Council of the First International, Minutes 1870-1871* (Moscow: Progress Publishers, 1974), 258.
17. MECW, 8:365. See MECW, 6:527 for a similar and somewhat more insightful comment made in 1847. Note also Marx and Engels's comment cited above, about the import of the California discovery.
18. MECW, 19:36-37. In an otherwise faithful and sympathetic reading of their views, Jeffrey Vogel fails to note this reassessment. Jeffrey Vogel, "The Tragedy of History," *New Left Review*, vol. 1, no. 220 (November–December 1996): 40–41, https://newleftreview.org/issues/i220/articles/jeffrey-vogel-the-tragedy-of-history.
19. Les Terry, " 'Not a Postmodern Nomad': A Conversation with Stuart Hall on Race, Ethnicity and Identity," *Arena Journal*, vol. 5: 56–57.
20. Stuart Hall, "Gramsci's Relevance for the Study of Race and Ethnicity," *Journal of Communication Inquiry*, vol. 10: 15.
21. MECW, 41:453.
22. MECW, 41:4, 7.
23. MECW, 43:429.
24. MECW, 40:344.
25. See Henry Collins and Chimen Abramsky, *Karl Marx and the British Labour Movement: Years of the First International* (New York: Macmillan, 1965), 59–81 for details on the composition and limitations of the British trade union participation in the IWMA.
26. *The Hague Congress of the First International, September 2–7, 1872: Minutes and Documents* (Moscow: Progress Publishers, 1976), 124.
27. MECW, 45:18. For evidence that substantiates Marx's charges, see Collins and Abramsky, *Karl Marx and the British Labour Movement*, 260; Royden Harrison, *Before the Socialists: Studies in Labour and Politics, 1861–1881* (Toronto: University of Toronto Press, 1965), chap. 4.
28. MECW, 23:613. In their otherwise useful discussion of the difficulties of the

IWMA in England, Collins and Abramsky unfortunately do not address this factor.

29. MECW, 47:55.
30. MECW, 43:390.
31. Ibid. Italics in original.
32. Maximilien Rubel, *Marx without Myth* (New York: Harper and Row, 1975), 252.
33. MECW, 43:424.
34. MECW, 43:450. In 1870 Marx foresaw that a war with Germany would be "the midwife of the inevitable social revolution in Russia" (MECW, 44;57).
35. MECW, 45:103. I am referring, of course, to the revolutionary upheavals in Germany that followed in the wake of the Russian Revolution in 1917.
36. *The General Council of the First International, 1868–1870, Minutes* (Moscow: Progress Publishers, 1974), 220.
37. MECW, 24:200.
38. Ibid.
39. MECW, 24:359.
40. MECW, 24:371.
41. MECW, 24:50.
42. MECW, 45:296.
43. MECW, 24:103.
44. MECW, 46:198. Italics in original.
45. Also noteworthy is the fact that Marx spent his final years reading and taking notes on pre-capitalist societies from the Americas to Europe and Asia—giving the lie once again to the Eurocentric charge. For details see Lawrence Krader, *The Ethnological Notebooks of Karl Marx* (Assen, The Netherlands: Van Gorcum, 1972).
46. MECW, 27:433.
47. Volume 47 of the *Collected Works* is the most accessible record. For the more ambitious, the projected 114-volume *Marx-Engels Gesamtausgabe* (*MEGA*) (Amsterdam: Internationale Marx-Engels-Stiftung (IMES) which is about half completed, is the definitive account. All 50 volumes are now in print.
48. August H. Nimtz, "Marxism," *The Oxford Companion to Politics of the World* (New York: Oxford University Press, 1993), 569–75.

4. Marx on Race: What the Critics Get Wrong

1. Cedric J. Robinson, *Black Marxism: The Making of the Black Radical Tradition* (London: Zed Books, 1983), 290.
2. August H. Nimtz and Kyle A. Edwards, *The Communist and the Revolutionary Liberal in the Second American Revolution: Comparing Karl Marx and Frederick Douglass in Real-Time* (Leiden, The Netherlands: Brill, 2024); the paperback edition, with the same title, is Chicago: Haymarket Press, 2025.

3. Richard Enmale, ed., *Karl Marx and Friedrich Engels, The Civil War in the United States* (New York: International Publishers, 1937); A. Zimmerman, "Introduction," in *The Civil War in the United States, Karl Marx and Frederick Engels* (New York: International Publishers, 2016), xxvi. Except for an article or two in the *Marx-Engels Collected Works* (New York: International Publishers, 1975–2004), hereafter MECW, the only thing missing is an index, given the richness of the materials.
4. For a defense of Marx on the broader topics of "Nationalism, Imperialism, and Race," see, most recently, China Miéville, *A Spectre Haunting: On the Communist Manifesto* (Chicago: Haymarket Books, 2022), 113–30.
5. August Nimtz, *Marx, Tocqueville, and Race in America: The 'Absolute Democracy' or 'Defiled Republic'* (Lanham, MD: Lexington Books, 2003), 131–32n35.
6. Zimmerman, "Introduction," in *The Civil War in the United States, Karl Marx and Frederick Engels*, xxvi.
7. Karl Marx and Friedrich Engels, MECW, 41:346. See also, Gregory Slack, "Did Marx Defend Black Slavery? On Jamaica and Labour in Black Skin," *Historical Materialism*, Vol. 31, No. 3 (2023). Italics in original.
8. Henry Charles Carey, *The Slave Trade, Domestic and Foreign: Why It Exists and How It May Be Extinguished* (Woodbridge Township, NJ: Project Gutenberg, 2005), https://www.gutenberg.org/cache/epub/8000/pg8000-images.html; John Bellamy Foster, Hannah Holleman, and Brett Clark convincingly argue, contrary to some claims, that Marx was well informed on the slavery question before the publication of Carey's book in 1853. Foster et al., "Marx and Slavery," *Monthly Review*, Vol. 72, No.3 (July/August 2020), https://monthlyreview.org/2020/07/01/marx-and-slavery/.
9. David Blight, *Frederick Douglass: Prophet of Freedom* (New York: Simon & Schuster, 2018), xvii.
10. Manisha Sinha, *The Slave's Cause: A History of Abolition* (New Haven: Yale University Press, 2016), 426.
11. Zimmerman, "Introduction," xxvi–xxvii. Zimmerman previewed her main complaint a year earlier in A. Zimmerman, "From the Second American Revolution to the First International and Back Again: Marxism, the Popular Front, and the American Civil War," in *The World the Civil War Made*, ed. Gregory P. Downs and Kate Masur (Chapel Hill: University of North Carolina Press, 2015). For a persuasive refutation of her claim that Marx and Engels regarded the war not as a "bourgeois revolution but a workers' revolution," 317, see Brian Kelly, "Slave Self-Activity and the Bourgeois Revolution in the United States: Jubilee and the Boundaries of Black Freedom," *Historical Materialism*, Vol. 27, No.3 (2019).
12. As in Ryan Grim's painfully revealing "The Elephant in the Zoom," *The Intercept*, June 13, 2022, https://theintercept.com/2022/06/13/progressive-organizing-infighting-callout-culture/.

13. James Oakes, *Freedom National: The Destruction of Slavery in the United States, 1861–1865* (New York: W. W. Norton, 2013), xiv.
14. August Nimtz, *The Ballot, the Streets, or Both? From Marx and Engels to Lenin and the October Revolution* (Chicago: Haymarket Books, 2019), 91.
15. MECW, 46:77.
16. John Blassingame, ed., *The Frederick Douglass Papers: Series One: Speeches, Debates, and Interviews*, Vol. 3:1855–63 (New Haven: Yale University Press, 1985), 467.
17. Douglass's *Monthly*, February 1863, 785.
18. Nimtz and Edwards, *The Communist and the Revolutionary Liberal,* 35.
19. Ibid., 49–50.
20. Ibid., 82–83.
21. As Oakes argues, the "transfer of the labor services of half a million black workers from the masters who owned them to the Unionists who employed them as wage laborers was the essence of the revolution we call emancipation, a revolution that was indispensable to Union victory." James Oakes, "Du Bois's 'General Strike,'" NONsite.org, No. 28, May 10, 2019, https://nonsite.org/duboiss-general-strike/.
22. Most recently, Oakes, "Du Bois's 'General Strike.'" Also, George Novack, *America's Revolutionary Heritage* (Atlanta, GA: Pathfinder Press, 2013), 345–57; and Jack Barnes, *Malcolm X, Black Liberation & the Road to Workers Power* (Atlanta, GA: Pathfinder Press, 2009), 157–69, 370–74.
23. Frederick Sorge, Marx and Engels's next closest contact in the United States after Weydemeyer's death in 1866, indicated to them in June 1871 that the Republican Party's hold on Blacks was a major political obstacle to Black/white working-class unity. Nimtz, *Marx, Tocqueville, and Race in America,* 153. Apparently, Marx didn't fully appreciate Sorge's point.
24. Wulf Hund, "Marx and Haiti: Note on a Blank Space," *Journal of World Philosophies,* Vol. 6, No. 2 (Winter 2021).
25. Ibid., 76. For Charles Mills, Marx is one of the major political philosophers who is of "limited use in theorizing about the polity of 'white supremacy.'" See Charles Mills, *Black Visible: Essays on Philosophy and Race* (Ithaca, NY: Cornell University Press, 1998), 126.
26. MECW, 9:211.
27. Nimtz, *Marx, Tocqueville, and Race in America,* 52.
28. Hund, "Marx and Haiti," 80.
29. Also instructive is what Douglass said to a largely white audience in October 1864: "My white fellow-citizens: Let me defend you from your friends. You belong to the best branch of the Indo-caucasian race; you belong to the Anglo-Saxon branch of the great human family. The world is rocked by your power, and filled with your achievements. To the civilization of the nineteenth-century, your race is the main spring." John Blassingame and John R.

McKivigan, eds., *The Frederick Douglass Papers: Series One: Speeches, Debates, and Interviews,* vol. 4: *1864–80* (New Haven: Yale University Press, 1991), 47.

30. MECW, 4:119.
31. MECW, 6:303–4.
32. A recent example of this kind of treatment of Marx, excessive in fact, is Sara-Maria Sorentino, "The Abstract Slave: Anti-Blackness and Marx's Method," *International Labor and Working Class History,* No. 96 (Fall 2019), https://www.cambridge.org/core/journals/international-labor-and-working-class-history/article/abs/abstract-slave-antiblackness-and-marxs-method/7B3A9767C4E84064E43DCD350DB68992.
33. MECW, 24:468.
34. W. E. B. Du Bois, *Black Reconstruction in America, 1860–1880: Introduction by David Levering Lewis* (New York: Free Press, 1998), 700. Also, Adolph Reed, Jr., "Du Bois and the 'Wages of Whiteness'": What He Meant, What He Didn't, and, Besides, It Shouldn't Matter for Our Politics Anyway," NONsite.org, June 29, 2017, https://nonsite.org/du-bois-and-the-wages-of-whiteness/.
35. For the best account of the class divisions in the Confederacy and their significance, see Bruce Levine, *The Fall of the House of Dixie: The Civil War and the Social Revolution that Transformed the South* (New York: Random House, 2013).
36. "grounded in material reality" replaces "apprehensible" in the original.
37. MECW, 24:200.
38. David S. Reynolds, *John Brown, Abolitionist: The Man Who Killed Slavery, Sparked the Civil War, and Seeded Civil Rights* (New York: Alfred Knopf, 2005), 107–10. Especially, 108: "The society of blacks that was by far the greatest inspiration for John Brown was the one created in Haiti by Toussaint L'Ouverture."
39. MECW, 41:4.
40. Nimtz and Edwards, *The Communist and the Revolutionary Liberal,* 40–41.
41. Hal Draper, *Karl Marx's Theory of Revolution,* Vol. 1: *State and Bureaucracy* (New York: Monthly Review Press, 1977), 591–608. More recently, see Shlomo Avineri, *Karl Marx: Philosophy and Revolution* (New Haven: Yale University Press, 2019), 41–54.
42. MECW, 41:389–90.
43. Nimtz, *Marx, Tocqueville, and Race in America,* 132n35.
44. MECW, 41:556.
45. See also Gareth Stedman Jones, *Karl Marx: Greatness and Illusion* (Boston: Harvard University Press, 2016), 165–67, 444; Jonathan Sperber, *Karl Marx: A Nineteenth Century Life* (New York: W. W. Norton, 2013), 409–14.
46. MECW, 43:474–75.
47. MECW, 43:398.

48. MECW, 43:390.
49. Regarding the lessons of the Commune, see Nimtz, *Marx and Engels: Their Contribution to the Democratic Breakthrough* (Albany, NY: SUNY Press, 2000), 215–16.
50. Hund, "Marx and Haiti," 89.
51. W. E. B. Du Bois, "Karl Marx and the Negro," in A. Zimmerman, ed., *The Civil War in the United States, Karl Marx and Frederick Engels,* 219.
52. Hund, "Marx and Haiti," 89.
53. Ibid., 90.
54. MECW, 11:103.
55. Hund, "Marx and Haiti," 98.
56. Ibid., 98n102.
57. Abram Leon, *The Jewish Question: A Marxist Interpretation* (Atlanta, GA: Pathfinder Press, 2020), 41.
58. August Nimtz, "From a Constituent of Congresswoman Ilhan Omar on Anti-Semitism: What It Is and Why It's Dangerous," *Tikkun,* May 8, 2019, https://www.tikkun.org/from-a-constituent-of-congresswoman-ilhan-omar -on-anti-semitism/.
59. Vladimir I. Lenin, *Collected Works* (Moscow: Progress Publishers, 1977), 437–42.
60. Jack Barnes, *Malcolm X, Black Liberation & the Road to Workers Power,* 243.
61. John Riddell, ed., *Workers of the World and Oppressed Peoples, Unite!: Proceedings and Documents of the Second Congress, 1920,* Vol. 1 (New York: Pathfinder Press, 1991), 286–87. "Racism" was not the term Lenin employed in his comment but added later. "National chauvinism" would likely have been his usage. Thanks to Susie Day and Arun Kundnani for pointing this out.
62. Barnes, *Malcolm X, Black Liberation & the Road to Workers Power,* 247.
63. Ibid., 265.
64. Ibid., 281.
65. Leon Trotsky, *Writings of Leon Trotsky, 1938–39* (New York: Pathfinder Press, 1974), 298–89.
66. Barnes, *Malcolm X, Black Liberation & the Road to Workers Power,* 295.
67. James Cannon, *The First Ten Years of American Communism: Report of a Participant* (New York: Lyle Stuart, 1962), 233.
68. Andrew J. Douglas and Jared A. Loggins, *Prophet of Discontent: Martin Luther King Jr. and the Critique of Racial Capitalism* (Athens, GA: University of Georgia Press, 2021), 6.
69. See chapter 5 for details.
70. Douglas and Loggins, *Prophet of Discontent,* 23
71. Oliver Cox's 1948 *Caste, Class and Race,* an example of the Black radical tradition for Robinson, could be argued to have been the first. Critiquing Marx,

or better, correcting him, is, however, unlikely for Robinson, a minor theme with Cox. Oliver Cox, *Caste, Race, and Caste* (Modern Reader, 1948).

72. Robin D. G. Kelley, "What Did Cedric Robinson Mean by Racial Capitalism?" *Boston Review*, January 12, 2017, https://www.bostonreview.net/articles/robin-d-g-kelley-introduction-race-capitalism-justice/.
73. August H. Nimtz, "The Eurocentric Marx and Engels and other related myths," in *Marxism, Modernity, and Postcolonial Studies*, ed. Crystal Bartolovich and Neil Lazarus (New York: Cambridge University Press, 2002).
74. A good place to begin with for Lenin, real-time analysis, is his 1907 critique of German social democracy on the colonial question. *Lenin Collected Works*, Vol. 13, 82–93 (London: Lawrence & Wishart, 1969), https://archive.org/details/lenincollectedwo0013unse. As for Stalinism, Trotsky's 1936 classic, *The Revolution Betrayed*, remains the best explanation for the Stalinist counterrevolution in Russia. Leon Trotsky, *The Revolution Betrayed: What Is the Soviet Union and Where Is It Going?* (New York: Pathfinder Press, 1970).
75. Cebric J. Robinson, *Black Marxism*, 450.
76. Robinson, *Black Marxism*, 389, reveals that Robinson certainly knew about C. L. R. James's discussion with Trotsky and the account published by the SWP's publishing arm, Pathfinder Press.
77. Mills, *Black Visible*, 36–37.
78. Michael Dawson, "The Life and Work of Charles Mills," Center for the Humanities, April 29, 2022, Hear the interview that Dawson did with Mills, https://www.centerforthehumanities.org/programming/the-life-and-work-of-charles-mills.
79. See Gregory Slack, "From Class to Race and Back Again: A Critique of Charles Mills' Black Radical Liberalism," *Science & Society*, Vol. 84, No. 1 (January 2020), for a most informed critique of Mills.
80. Charles Mills, *The Racial Contract* (Ithaca, NY: Cornell University Press, 1997), 94.
81. We are indebted to Professor Igor Shoikhedbrod, https://www.stfx.ca/faculty-staff/igor-shoikhedbrod, for this insightful point.
82. Charles Mills, "Getting Out of the Cave: Tension between Democracy and Elitism in Marx's Theory of Cognitive Liberation," *Social and Economic Studies*, Vol. 39, No. (March 1990), 23–46. Also, August H. Nimtz, "The Making and Unmaking of a Revolution: Some Lessons from Grenada," *The African Review* [Dar es Salaam], Vol. 12, No. 2 (1985).
83. MECW, 5:236.
84. MECW, 6:343–44.
85. August H. Nimtz, "Why There Are No George Floyds in Cuba," *Legal Form*, June 17, 2020, https://legal form/blog/2020/06/17/why-there-are-no-george-floyds-in-cuba-august-h-nimtz/.
86. See chapter 5 for details.

87. A comparison of how Cuba and the United States dealt with the natural phenomena of hurricanes in the summer of 2005, specifically Hurricane Katrina, offers further evidence to verify this claim. See August H. Nimtz, "Natural versus Social Phenomena: Cuba and the Lessons of Katrina," *The Black Scholar*, Vol. 36, No. 4 (Winter, 2006).
88. Nelson Mandela and Fidel Castro, *How Far We Slaves Have Come! South Africa and Cuba in Today's World* (New York: Pathfinder Press, 1991), 20.
89. For the authoritative account, see Piero Gleijeses, *Visions of Freedom: Havana, Washington, Pretoria, and the Struggle for Southern Africa, 1976–1991* (Chapel Hill: University of North Carolina Press, 2013).
90. MECW, 6:351–52.

5. Revisiting *Black Marxism* Four Decades Later: Bringing Marx into the Class-versus-Race Debate

1. Exemplifying that debate, as this is being written, is Timothy Shenk's *New York Times* essay "Democrats Are in Crisis: Eat-the-Rich Populism Is the Only Answer," the first installment, the *Times* editors write, "in a series on the thinkers, upstarts and ideologues battling for control of the Democratic Party." October 5, 2025.
2. Michael Roberts's *The Long Depression* continues to be the most comprehensive explanation. See *The Long Depression: How It Happened, Why It Happened, and What Happens Next* (Chicago: Haymarket Books, 2016). More recently, see Patricia Cohen, "Why It Seems that Everything We Knew About the Global Economy is No Longer True," *New York Times*, June 18, 2023, https://www.nytimes.com/2023/06/18/business/economy/global-economy-us-china.html; Aaron Benanav, "There's a Reason the World Is a Mess, and It's Not Trump," *New York Times*, April 21, 2025, https://www.nytimes.com/2025/04/21/opinion/trump-tariffs-global-economy.html.
3. Marc James Léger, ed., *Identify Trumps Socialism: The Class and Identity Debate after Neoliberalism* (New York: Routledge, 2023).
4. Gregory Slack, "Did Marx Defend Black Slavery?" *Historical Materialism/Research in Critical Marxist Theory*, Vol. 31, Nos. 2 & 3 (2023), https://www.historicalmaterialism.org/journal/issue-3123-race-and-capital-2/.
5. Most recently, see Andrew J. Douglas and Jared A. Loggins, *Prophet of Discontent: Martin Luther King Jr. and the Critique of Racial Capitalism* (Athens: University of Georgia Press, 2021), 5–6. Also, Wolf Hund, "Marx and Haiti: Note on a Blank Space," *Journal of World Philosophies* 6 (Winter 2021): 76. Earlier, see Charles Mills, *The Racial Contract* (Ithaca, NY: Cornell University Press, 1998), 126.
6. I'm indebted to Robert Nichols, who also makes that charge, for that admission. Robert Nichols, *The Theft Is Property! Dispossession and Critical Theory* (Durham, NC: Duke University Press, 2019), 134.

7. The comparison doesn't rest on any direct Marx-Douglass interaction or consciousness about one another. Douglass no doubt read Marx who occasionally wrote for the *New York Daily Tribune*, which he assiduously read. As for the likelihood of Marx having read Douglass, see August H. Nimtz and Kyle A. Edwards, *The Communist and the Revolutionary Liberal in the Second American Revolution: Comparing Karl Marx and Frederick Douglass in Real-Time* (Leiden: Brill, 2024), 212–13.
8. Karl Marx and Friedrich Engels, *Collected Works* (New York: International Publishers, 1975–2004), Vol. 4, 119; hereafter MECW.
9. MECW, 5:114. Even a sympathetic biography, Sven-Eric Liedman's *A World to Win: The Life and Work of Karl Marx* (London: Verso, 2018), could only manage to devote at best a page and a footnote to Marx's Civil War actions in its almost 800 pages. Raymond Geuss's discussion of Marx's views on how to end slavery would have benefited from an examination of Marx's actual analysis/practice in regard to the institution in the United States, as we do in our Marx-Douglass book. See Geuss, "The Moral Legacy of Marxism," *Analyse & Kritik* (Stuttgart, DE: January 2, 2015), 63.
10. For some useful details about the incident, see https://citystoriesucla.github.io/lyricalmap/article/2016-09-01-f16-07. See also Ward Churchill and Jim Vander Wall, *Agents of Repression: The FBI's Secret Wars Against the Black Panther Party and the American Indian Movement* (Boston: South End Press, 1990).
11. Cedric J. Robinson, "Preface," in *Black Marxism: The Making of the Black Radical Tradition* (Chapel Hill, NC: University of North Carolina Press, 2000), xlviii–xlvx. Italics added.
12. MECW, 1:160, 162, 167.
13. MECW, 3:153. Italics added.
14. Frederick Douglass and John W. Blassingame, *The Frederick Douglass Papers, Series One: Speeches, Debates, and Interviews,* vol 1: *1841–46* (New Haven: Yale University Press, 1979), 81.
15. MECW, 6:167.
16. MECW, 8:211. Marx's point enables a critique of Robinson's charge about Marx's supposed blinders on the race question. See Michael Ralph and Maya Singhal, "Racial Capitalism," *Theory and Society* 48 (December 20, 2019): n. 21.
17. MECW, 6:325.
18. MECW, 6:344.
19. Engels's distinction, so relevant here, did not make it into Marx's final version of the *Manifesto*. MECW, 6:495.
20. Hal Draper, *The Adventures of the Communist Manifesto* (Alameda, CA: Center for Socialist History, 1994), 231.
21. Charles H. George, *500 Years of Revolution: European Radicals from Hus to Lenin* (Chicago: Charles H. Kerr, 1998), 99–110.

22. Draper, *The Adventures of the Communist Manifesto*, 315.
23. MECW, 6:496, 504, 519.
24. In hindsight, Raymond Geuss's *Philosophy and Real Politics* (Princeton: Princeton University Press, 2008) was also an inspiration.
25. MECW, 19:30.
26. Charles Mill, *The Racial Contract* (Ithaca, N.Y.: Cornell University Press, 1997), 94.
27. MECW, 41:277.
28. MECW, 19:14.
29. Ibid.
30. See Elizabeth Varon, *Armies of Deliverance: A New History of the Civil War* (Oxford: Oxford University Press, 2019), 15–16; and Bruce Levine, *Half Slave and Half Free: The Roots of Civil War*, rev. ed. (New York: Hill and Wang, 2005), 247.
31. MECW, 19:264. "Marx uses the English word," according to the *Collected Works* editors. For details on Marx and Engels's usage of the N-word, see Nimtz and Edwards, *The Communist and the Revolutionary Liberal in the Second American Revolution* (Boston: Brill, 2024), 10–12.
32. MECW, 20:20.
33. MECW, 41:305.
34. Du Bois estimates that in 1860 only 11 percent of Blacks were "free workers," or about 1 percent of the entire working class. W. E. B. Du Bois, *Black Reconstruction: An Essay Towards the History of the Part which Black Folk Played in the Attempt to Reconstruct America, 1860–1880* (New York: Library of America, 1992), 7.
35. John Blassingame, ed., *The Frederick Douglass Papers, Series One: Speeches, Debates, and Interviews*, vol. 3: *1855–63* (New Haven: Yale University Press, 1985), 562–63.
36. MECW, 42:163.
37. MECW, 42:167.
38. Angela [Andrew] Zimmerman, *The Civil War in the United States: Karl Marx and Frederick Engels* (New York: International Publishers, 2016), 167–75.
39. Eric Foner, *Reconstruction: America's Unfinished Revolution, 1863–1877* (New York: Harper and Row, 1988), 584, passim for details about the strike.
40. MECW, 45:251.
41. George Frederickson, *White Supremacy: A Comparative Study in American and South African History* (New York: Oxford University Press, 1981), 62–63.
42. Henry Louis Gates, ed., *Frederick Douglass: Autobiographies* (New York: Library of America, 1994), 177–78.
43. Foner, *Reconstruction*, 544–45.
44. Nimtz and Edwards, *The Communist and the Revolutionary Liberal in the Second American Revolution*, 257–58.

45. Marya McQuirter, "31 march 1968 & martin luther king, jr speaks at national cathedral," blog, *dc1968: 365 stories re washington dc in 1968*, https://www.dc1968project.com/blog/2018/3/31/31-march-1968-mlk-speaks -at-national-cathedral.
46. Karl Marx, *Capital, Volume 1* (New York: International Publishers, 1972), 301.
47. MECW, 43: 398.
48. Heather Cox Richardson, *The Death of Reconstruction: Race, Labor and Politics in the Post–Civil War North, 1865–1901* (Boston: Harvard University Press, 2001).
49. MECW, 23:175.
50. For how Douglass read the Commune very differently from Lenin, see Kyle A. Edwards, "'Those Deluded, Ill-Starred Men': Frederick Douglass, the New National Era, and the Paris Commune," *New North Star*, Vol. 4, No. 1 (December 19, 2022): 1–19, https://doi.org/10.18060/26926. Nimtz and Edwards, *The Communist and the Revolutionary Liberal in the Second American Revolution*, Appendix A: Regarding the Paris Commune and Lenin; also see August H. Nimtz, "'The Bolsheviks Come to Power': A New Interpretation," *Science & Society*, Vol. 81/4: 478-500.
51. MECW, 50:236.
52. Whether Du Bois got Marx right has been the subject of discussions ever since. See George Novack, *America's Revolutionary Heritage* (Atlanta, GA: Pathfinder Press, 2013), 353–54; Brian Kelly, "Slave Self-Activity and the Bourgeois Revolution in the United States: Jubilee and the Boundaries of Black Freedom," *Historical Materialism*, Vol. 27, No. 3 (2019): and James Oakes, "Du Bois's 'General Strike,'" No. 28, May 10, 2019, https://nonsite.org/duboiss-general-strike/. For purposes here, I focus on the non-contentious aspects of Du Bois's reading of Marx. Regarding Du Bois's acknowledged debt to Marx, see Nimtz and Edwards, *The Communist and the Revolutionary Liberal in the Second American Revolution*, 301–2.
53. Nikole Hannah-Jones, Caitlin Roper, Ilena Silverman, Jake Silverstein, *The 1619 Project* (New York: One World, 2021), 465. The 2019 version appears in *The New York Times Magazine*, https://www.nytimes.com/interactive/2019/08/14/magazine/1619-america-slavery.html.
54. Jamelle Bouie, "Why I Keep Coming Back to Reconstruction," *New York Times*, October 25, 2022.
55. Anne Case and Angus Deaton, *Deaths of Despair and the Future of Capitalism* (Princeton: Princeton University Press, 2020).
56. August Nimtz, "The Graveyard of Progressive Social Movements: The Black Hole of the Democratic Party," provides details, *MR Online*, May 9, 2017, https://mronline.org/2017/05/09/the-graveyard-of-progressive-social -movements/.

57. "Today, just over half of the country still believes the [American] dream is possible, according to a 2024 Pew Research Center survey: Americans are split over the state of the American dream," Gabriel Borrelli, *Pew Research Center,* July 2, 2024, https://www.pewresearch.org/short-reads/2024/07/02/americans-are-split-over-the-state-of-the-american-dream/. Another 41 percent said the dream was no longer achievable, and 6 percent said it was never possible. Audra D. S. Burch, "What Has Happened to the American Dream?," *New York Times,* May 3, 2025, https://www.nytimes.com/interactive/2025/05/04/us/trump-american-dream-voters.html.
58. MECW, 20:20.
59. MECW, 46:153. Thanks to Kyle Edwards for locating Engels's so timely point.
60. Brooke Gladstone, "What Media Coverage of Trump's Movement Is Missing," interview with Jeff Sharlet, *On the Media,* June 16, 2023, https://www.wnycstudios.org/podcasts/otm/segments/what-media-coverage-trump-movement-missing-on-the-media. For a detailed analysis of the vote that disputes the racist thesis, see Thomas Ferguson et al., "The Roots of Right-Wing Populism: Donald Trump in 2016," *International Journal of Political Economy,* Vol. 49, No. 2 (2020), https://doi.org/10.1080/08911916.2020.1778861. My 2016 article, "A Black Socialist in Trump Country," was my first effort to challenge liberal assumptions about Trump voters; see *Minneapolis Star Tribune,* July 29, 2016, https://www.startribune.com/a-black-socialist-in-trump-country/388716201.
61. August H. Nimtz, *The Ballot, the Streets, or Both? From Marx and Engels to Lenin and the October Revolution* (Chicago: Haymarket Books, 2019), 63.
62. August H. Nimtz, Jr., "It's a big deal that the outrage expressed over George Floyd's death was massive and multiracial," *Minnpost,* May 28, 2020: https://www.minnpost.com/community-voices/2020/05/its-a-big-deal-that-the-outrage-expressed-over-george-floyds-death-was-massive-and-multiracial/.
63. For details and visuals, see Tina Burnside, "Duluth Lynchings," *Minnesota Historical Society,* July 22, 2019, https://www.mnopedia.org/event/duluth-lynchings.
64. George J. Sanchez, "Reginald Denny: The Politics of Whiteness in the Late Twentieth Century" *American Quarterly* 47/3 (September 1995).
65. Wesley Lowery's *America Backlash: A Changing Nation and the Cost of Progress* (New York: HarperCollins, 2023), is the latest edition of this claim. The attention and sales the book has garnered, as of this writing, suggests that the thesis still has shelf life. See my critique of the author who initiated this campaign: "The Meritocratic Myopia of Ta-Nehisi Coates," *MR Online,* November 17, 2017, https://mronline.org/2017/11/17/the-meritocratic-myopia-of-ta-nehisi-coates/.
66. August H. Nimtz, "The real flaw in CRT is that it's not revolutionary

enough," *The Minnesota Star Tribune,* November 17, 2021: https://www.startribune.com/counterpoint-the-real-flaw-in-crt-is-that-its-not-revolutionary-enough/600117931.

67. See August H. Nimtz, "The Chauvin Verdict: A historic victory that points the way forward," *MR Online,* May 2, 2021, https://mronline.org/2021/05/02/the-chauvin-verdict-a-historic-victory-that-points-the-way-forward/.
68. Martin Luther King, Jr., "Where Do We Go from Here?" Stanford University, Martin Luther King, Jr. Research and Education Institute, https://kinginstitute.stanford.edu/where-do-we-go-here. The speech is conspicuously absent in Peniel E. Joseph's *The Sword and the Shield: The Revolutionary Lives of Malcolm X and Martin Luther King Jr.* (New York: Basic Books, 2020), 60, but it provides evidence that King did read what he claimed when a student at Crozer Theological Seminary in Chester, Pennsylvania.
69. Peter Dreier, "A True and Visionary Radical, Martin Luther King, Jr. Was No Moderate," *Countercurrents.Org,* January 17, 2023: http://countercurrents.org/2023/01/a-true-and-visionary-radical-martin-luther-king-jr-was-no-moderate/; David McNally, "It's Called Capitalism: Naming the System Behind Systemic Racism: An Interview with Keeanga-Yamahtta Taylor," *Spectre Journal,* June 1, 2022, https://spectrejournal.com/its-called-capitalism-naming-the-system-behind-systemic-racism/. See also the most recent and authoritative biography by Jonathan Eig, *King: A Life* (New York: Macmillan, 2023), 480–81.
70. Martin Luther King, Jr., "The Role of the Behavioral Scientist in the Civil Rights Movement," *Journal of Social Issues,* Vol. 74, No. 1 (1968), 220. See American Psychological Association for text, https://www.apa.org/monitor/features/king-challenge.
71. About the key finds of the research King referred to, see Nimtz and Edwards, *The Communist and the Revolutionary Liberal,* 303.
72. Andrew J. Douglas and Jared A. Loggins, *Prophet of Discontent: Martin Luther King Jr. and the Critique of Racial Capitalism* (Athens: University of Georgia Press, 2021), 23.
73. Peniel Joseph makes that claim in his *The Sword and the Shield,* in the Epilogue.
74. Exactly what Jack Barnes makes a credible case for; see Barnes, *Malcolm X, Black Liberation & the Road to Workers Power* (Atlanta, GA: Pathfinder Press, 2009), 358–59.
75. Cedric J. Robinson, *Black Marxism,* 450. That he helped bring Malcolm X to the Berkeley campus in 1963 makes the absence even more remarkable. See Robin D. G. Kelley, "What Did Cedric Robinson Mean by Racial Capitalism," *Boston Review,* January 12, 2017, https://www.bostonreview.net/articles/robin-d-g-kelley-introduction-race-capitalism-justice/.
76. "There will be a clash between the oppressed and the oppressors," from

Marlene Nadle's interview with Malcolm X in *Last Answers and Interviews* (New York: Pathfinder Press, 1965), excerpted in *The Militant,* September 30, 2019, Vol. 83, No. 25, 9, https://themilitant.com/2019/09/21/there-will-be-a-clash-between-the-oppressed-and-the-oppressors/.

77. Jan Carew, *Ghosts in Our Blood: With Malcolm X in Africa, England, and the Caribbean* (Chicago: Lawrence Hill Books, 1994), 36. Malcolm ended his point with a chillingly accurate forecast of his fate ten days later.
78. On that history, see my essay "The Graveyard of Progressive Social Movements: The Black Hole of the Democratic Party," *MR Online,* May 9, 2017.
79. August H. Nimtz, "The Trump Moment: Why It Happened, Why We 'Dodged the Bullet', and 'What Is To Be Done,'" *Legal Form,* February 24, 2021: https://legalform.blog/2021/02/24/the-trump-moment-why-it-happened-why-we-dodged-the-bullet-and-what-is-to-be-done-august-h-nimtz/.
80. See, for example, https://www.epi.org/publication/major-strike-activity-in-2023/.
81. Nimtz, "Trump Redux: A Silver Lining?" *Legal Form,* December 6, 2024: https://legalform.blog/2024/12/06/trump-redux-august-nimtz/. Kyle A. Edwards makes the case for independent working-class political action in his introduction to a speech Benjamin Butler gave in support of the Paris Commune, reproduced in "Butler on the Paris Commune," *Cosmonaut,* January 3, 2025, https://cosmonautmag.com/2025/01/butler-on-the-paris-commune/.
82. Kudos to Cedric Johnson, "Wrong Durée: The Politics of Cedric J. Robinson's Racial Capitalism," Nonsite.org, January 29, 2025, https://nonsite.org/the-wrong-duree-the-politics-of-cedric-j-robinsons-racial-capitalism/, for picking up on what I pointed out.
83. See what continues to be the best political explanation for that counterrevolution: Steve Clark, "The Second Assassination of Maurice Bishop," *New International6* (New York: Pathfinder Press, 1987).
84. Only recently, when going through my African Liberation Support Committee files (now at the African Activists Archives, https://africanactivist.msu.edu/; https://africanactivist.msu.edu/search/results/?keyword=nimts), did I learn that Bishop and I were both ALSC members at the same time.
85. Keeanga-YamahttaTaylor: "It's Called Capitalism: Naming the System Behind Systemic Racism," *Spectre Journal,* June 1, 2022."
86. Maurice Bishop, *Maurice Bishop Speaks: The Grenada Revolution and Its Overthrow: 1973–1983* (New York: Pathfinder Press, 1986), 117–19.
87. I'm indebted to William Robinson et al., 2022, for this insight. Bedour Alagraa not only is mistaken about "a radio silence of critical reviews of the book . . . until 1988," but also fails to understand the political context as argued here for the poor reception the book garnered initially and why that

changed after Kelley's foreword to the 2000 edition. See "Cedric Robinson's Black Marxism: Thirty-Five Years Later," *CLR James Journal*, Vol. 24, No. 1–2 (Fall 2018).

88. "'Not just my comrade but my brother': Cornel West on Marx and Cedric Robinson," |Columbia Center for Contemporary Critical Thought, Marx 10/13, https://www.youtube.com/watch?v=Jt1hvsZcHSQ&t=2s, beginning at 49:13.
89. William Robinson et al., "The Cult of Cedric Robinson's *Black Marxism*: A Proletarian Critique," *The Philosophical Salon*, 3 October 2022, and "Take Two," *The Philosophical Salon*, 30 June 2025, provide examples.
90. See my contribution, "Stalinism," to the "Symposium on Stalinism" in *Science & Society*, Vol. 83, No. 3 (2019).
91. Rachel Wolfe, "The American Dream Feels out of Reach for Most," *Wall Street Journal*, August 28, 2024, https://www.wsj.com/economy/consumers/american-dream-poll-us-economy.. Also, Jared Abbott and René Rojas, "Democrats Lost Working-Class Voters' Trust," *Jacobin*, Dec. 27, 2025.
92. Of relevance is Fritz Backhaus et al., *Roads Not Taken, Or: Things Could Have Turned Out Differently: German Caesuras 1989–1848* (Munich: C.H. Beck, 2023) which brings together essays and graphics for a current exhibit.
93. MECW, 27: 245.
94. MECW, 48: 134-5.
95. V. I. Lenin, Collected Works (Moscow: Progress Publishers, 1960), Vol. 5, 18.
96. Robinson previewed his rejection of Marx's project in his 1980 book *The Terms of Order* which contested "the political" owing to its apparent Eurocentrism. See Rafael Kachaturian, "The Persistence of the Political: On Cedric J. Robinson's *The Terms of Order*" (*Polity*, Vol. 57, no. 3, July 2025). In contrast to William Robinson et al., 2022 and 2025, whose critique of *Black Marxism* focuses on Marx's theory, I prioritize Marx's practice to make my case, specifically, how he responded to the Second American Revolution.

Index

Abdelkader (Abd el-Kader), 65
Address to the Central Authority of 1850 (Marx and Engels), 52
African Americans, *see* Blacks
African Journal of Political Economy, 39
African Liberation Support Committee (ALSC), 35
African Socialism or Socialist Africa? (Babu), 43, 56–57
Algeria, 64–65
Allen, Robert, 39
Angola, 121
anti-apartheid movement, 25
anti-imperialist and anticolonial struggle, 50
antisemitism, 100–101; Lenin on, 110; Leon on, 106–7, 114
Arab Spring, 168
Arbery, Ahmaud, 153

Babbitt, Ashli, 150
Babu, A. M., 43, 56–57
Bacon, Nathaniel, 141
Ball, Jared, 9
Baraka, Amiri, 35
Beaumont, Gustave de, 96
Bishop, Maurice: Grenada Revolution led by, 161; on links between Black and white working class, 38, 57–58, 162, 165; omitted by Robinson, 12
Black Lives Matter movement, 153, 164
Black Marxism: The Making of the Black Radical Tradition (Robinson), 34, 60, 125–26; author's review of, 34–58; omission of Malcolm X from, 116–17, 157; people omitted from, 160–64; reviews of, 8–9; West on, 7
Black nationalism: of Malcolm X, 156; Robinson on, 83; SWP support for, 34–36, 113–14
Black Reconstruction (Du Bois), 91, 105, 145–46
Blacks: born into slavery, 84–85; class divisions among, 164; Louisiana's "one-drop rule" on, 21; Trotsky on, 111–13; in U.S. Foreign Service, 32; vote granted to, 140; in working class, 149–50
Boeing (firm), 148
Bohemian Caverns (nightclub, Washington, D.C.), 33
Bolsheviks (Russia), 108, 109

Bouie, Jamelle, 145–46
bourgeoisie, 52
Brown, John, 51, 100; Frederick Douglass on, 133; on Haitian Revolution, 99; Harpers Ferry rebellion by, 67, 88, 99
Brown v. Board of Education (U.S., 1954), 18–19, 144
Burns, Lizzie, 103
Bush, George W., 159

Cannon, James P., 110–13
Capital (Marx), 67–68, 98, 127; on hereditary proletariat in U.S., 147–48; published in Russian, 73; on slavery, 138; on U.S., post-Civil War, 142–43
capitalism: crises in, 42; racial capitalism, 116, 161, 162; Robinson on history of, 43–44; slavery tied to, 45–46; systemic racism as, 153
Carew, Jan, 158
Carey, Henry, 85–86
Carlson, Tucker, 159
Carmichael, Stokely (Kwame Toure), 25
Castro, Fidel, 23
Chartists, 69, 71
China, Taiping Rebellion in, 50, 63
civil rights movement, 23, 166; author's childhood participation in, 20; protests by, 151–52
Civil War (U.S.): Frederick Douglass on, 132, 138–39; Marx and Engels on, 16, 51, 52, 68, 84–88, 95, 134–35; John Stuart Mill on, 82; New Orleans during, 15
Civil War in France (Marx), 70, 143
classes: divisions among Blacks along, 164; tied to historical phases in the development of production, 42
colonialism, 51; Lenin on, 109
commodities, 44
Communards (Paris Commune), 70
communism: Marx and Engels on, 62–67; as movement, Engels on, 95
Communist League, 134
Communist Manifesto (Marx and Engels), 62, 80, 166, 167; addendum on Germany in, 64; on difference between proletarians and slaves, 118–19; on private property, 129–31; Russian edition of, 76; on slavery, 129; on taking state power, 150–51; on tasks for communists, 131
Communist Party (CPUSA), 17, 28, 35; as apologist for Soviet Union, 166; Du Bois in and on, 41, 53; on Malcolm X, 156–58; on race, 110
Cooper, Jake, 30
critical race theory, 152
Cuba, 22–23, 57, 120–21; Malcolm X on, 158

Davis, Angela, 28
Day, Susie, 9
DeBoer, Harry, 30
Debs, Eugene V., 109
Demands of the Communist Party of Germany, 64
Democratic Party, 158–60; during Civil War, 136–37; in election of 2024, 165; labor movement incorporated into, 166; Malcolm X on, 157

democratic socialism, 154–55
dictatorship of the proletariat, 42
Douglas, Andrew, 114–16
Douglass, Frederick, 11, 82, 117, 156; Brown and, 100, 133; on Confederate attack on Fort Sumter, 132; on emancipation of slaves and Civil War, 88–90; ignored by Robinson, 164; Marx compared with, 125–29; on nonslaveholding whites, 136, 138; on private property and Stevens, 140–42; on race, 94, 96–97; on racist counterrevolution, 105; on withdrawal of federal troops from South, 91
Draper, Hal, 100
Du Bois, W. E. B., 40–41; on Marx, 105; on psychological wage of white workers, 149; on Reconstruction, 145–46; Robinson on, 51–52, 81; on white working class, 97, 136; Zimmerman on, 91

Eastland, James, 16
education, segregation in, 18–19
Edwards, Kyle, 82, 83, 125
Eighteenth Brumaire (Marx), 52, 106
elections, presidential: of 1864, 137; of 1964, 24, 155, 157; of 2016, 150; of 2020, 153; of 2024, 123, 159, 165
Emancipation of Labor (Russia), 76
Emancipation Proclamation: final (1863), 89, 142; preliminary (1862), 90
Engels, Frederick, 9–10, 31; on Chartists, 69; on communism, 62–67, 95; on communist movement, 50; Frederick Douglass and, 141; Eurocentrism of, 60–61; on historical materialism, 41–42; Irish question and, 102–3; on lack of working-class party in U.S., 144, 158; nonwestern nationalism not understood by, 40; on parliamentary and electoral arenas, 155; on private property, 119, 129–31, 154; on the prospects for socialism in America, 147–48; on revolution in one country, 121; on Russia, 75–78; on slaves and slavery, 132–33; on U.S. Civil War, 52; wars predicted by, 167; Weydemeyer and, 139, 140; Zimmerman on, 84–91
England (Britain), 66; Ireland and Irish question for, 71–72, 102–3, 108, 143; revolutionary potential in, 69
Enmale, Richard, 84
Eurocentrism, 59; of Marx and Engels, 60–61, 66
European Spring (1848-1849), 82, 131–32, 139

Fanon, Frantz, 26–27, 41, 105
Fenians (Ireland), 26, 72, 108
Feuerbach, Ludwig, 154
First International, *See* International Working Men's Association
Flerovsky, N., 73
Floyd, George, 151, 153
Ford Foundation, 32
Fort Sumter, Confederate attack on, 99, 133; Brown's attack on Harpers Ferry leading to, 133;

Frederick Douglass on, 88–89, 132; Marx on, 92
France: Algeria under, 65; *see also* Paris Commune
Frazier, E. Franklin, 22

Garvey, Marcus, 55
general strike, 91
The German Ideology (Marx and Engels), 62, 118
Germany, 79; fascism in, 166; revolutionary movements in, 68; revolution of 1848 in, 64, 131–32
Geuss, Raymond, 132
Ghana, 23
Goldwater, Barry, 24, 157
Great Depression, 148
Great Railroad strike (1877), 141
Great Recession, 148
Grenada, 36–39; counterrevolution in, 118; omitted by Robinson, 56; Revolution in (1979), 12, 161, 162

Haiti, 91–92, 99, 106
Hall, Stuart, 66–67
Hammond, 96
Hansen, Emmanuel, 34, 39
Harris, Leonard, 8
Hayes, Rutherford B., 91
Hegel, Georg Wilhelm Friedrich, 62, 118, 154
Hendricks, Nathaniel, 19–20
historical materialism, Robinson on, 41–45, 127
Hopkins, Charles, 142
Hund, Wulf, 114, 116; on Marx, 91–95; on Marx's antisemitism, 99–107; on Marx's lack of theory of race, 146

India, 50, 65–66
industrialization, 44
industrial reserve army, 46
International Longshoremen's Association, 16–17
International Working Men's Association (IWMA; First International): Calcutta (India) branch of, 65–66; English trade unionists leave, 68; Irish question and, 108; Lincoln congratulated by, 137–38; Marx as head of, 102–3; on suffrage for former slaves, 140; trade unionists in, 69–71; during U.S. Civil War, 51
Iran, 162
Ireland and Irish question, 47–49; Frederick Douglass in, 97; IMWA on, 70; Lenin on, 107–8; Marx and Engels on, 71–72, 78–79, 102–3, 108–9, 143, 163–64

Jamaica, slavery in, 85–86
James, C. L. R., 40–41; on Haitian Revolution, 106; in SWP, 54–55; Trotsky meets with, 112–13; Trotsky's differences with, 56
Jews, antisemitism against, 100–101, 106–7
Jinadu, Adele, 34
Johnson, Andrew, 139, 142
Johnson, Lyndon, 24, 155, 157
Jones, Ernest, 69
Journal of African Marxists (JAM), 7–9, 38; author's review of *Black Marxism* published in, 34; founding of, 35

Kelley, Robin D. G., 8–9, 11–13, 115–16
King, Martin Luther, Jr.: Andrew Douglas and Loggins on, 114–15, 121–22; on land promised to former slaves, 142; on redistribution of economic and political power, 147, 153–55
King, Rodney, 152

Lafargue, Paul, 101
Lassalle, Ferdinand, 100–101
Léger, Marc James, 124
Lenin, Vladimir Ilich, 50, 76, 88; on Blacks and national question, 54, 56; death of, 111; Andrew Douglas and Loggins on, 115; on forming revolutionary organizations, 151, 168; on Hegel, 118; impact of Paris Commune on, 144; on Irish question and nationalism, 107–8, 164; on national and colonial questions, 109–10; Russian Revolution led by, 52
Leon, Abram, 106–7, 114
libraries, in New Orleans, 19–20
Lincoln, Abraham: Blacks admitted to Union Army under, 90; during Civil War, 95, 133; congratulated by International Working Men's Association, 137–38, 149; final Emancipation Proclamation issued by, 89, 142; as reader of *New York Daily Tribune,* 134
Loggins, Jared, 114–16
Louisiana, 21
L'Ouverture, Toussaint, 133
Luxemburg, Rosa, 107, 109

Malcolm X, 22, 26, 115, 151; assassination of, 160; Martin Luther King and, 155–56; on Marxism, 158; omitted from *Black Marxism,* 12, 116–17; SWP support for, 35, 114, 156–57
Malvinas/Falkland Islands, 48–49
Mandela, Nelson, 25, 120–21
Manifesto of the Communist Party (Marx and Engels), *see Communist Manifesto*
Martin, Trayvon, 153
Marx, Eleanor (daughter), 103
Marx, Karl, 9–10, 31; on anti-imperialist and anticolonial struggle, 50; on communism, 62–67; as correspondent for *New York Daily Tribune,* 134–35; debate between Frederick Douglass and, 11; Andrew Douglas and Loggins on, 114–15; Frederick Douglass compared with, 125–29; Du Bois on, 105; Eurocentrism of, 60–61; in First International, 69–71; on general law of capitalist accumulation, 46; Hund on, 91–95, 99–102, 106; on Irish question and racism, 47, 49, 163–64; Lincoln congratulated by, 137–38; Charles Mills on, 117–18; nonwestern nationalism not understood by, 40; on Paris Commune, 143–44; on parliamentary and electoral arenas, 155; on poor whites, 149; on predetermined circumstances, 15; on private property, 119, 129–31; on race, 124–25; on revolutionary movements, 68–69; on Russia, 72–78; on slaves and slavery, 89,

132–33; on U.S. Civil War, 16, 51, 52; on white working class, 136, 142; Zimmerman on, 84–91
Marx and Engels: Their Contribution to the Democratic Breakthrough (Nimtz), 163
Marx-Engels Collected Works (MECW), 59–60
Marxism: Malcolm X on, 158; Robinson on, 161, 168
McDonogh, 18
mechanization, 45–46
mercantile capitalism, 44, 45
Mexico, 66
The Militant (newspaper), 28–29, 31, 36–37
Mill, John Stuart, 82
Mills, Charles, 117–18, 132
Monk, Thelonious, 33

NAACP, in New Orleans, 17–18, 20
National Black Independent Political Party (NBIPP), 35–36
nationalism, 48; Lenin on, 107–8
national question, 54–56
National Reform Association, 131
Nation of Islam, 26, 156, 160
Negroes, *see* Blacks
neoliberalism, 163
New Jewel Movement (Grenada), 12, 161
New Orleans (Louisiana), author's childhood in, 15–22
New York City, 136–37
New York Daily Tribune (newspaper), 134–35
New York Times, 1619 Project of, 120, 141, 145, 152
Nicaragua, 36, 162
Nixon, Richard, 153
Nkomati Accord (South Africa-Mozambique security pact), 49
Northern Student Movement, 29

Oakes, James, 87
Obama, Barack, 152, 161
Obama administration, 152
O'Dell, Jack Pitts, 17

Paris Commune (1871), 64, 68, 70, 143–44
Pathfinder Press, 114
The Peasant Question in France and Germany (Engels), 64
peasantry, 64; in Russia, 76
Plekhanov, Georgi, 76
Plessy v. Ferguson (U.S., 1896), 105, 144
Poland, 67, 72
private property, 97–98, 120; *Communist Manifesto* on, 129–31; Frederick Douglass on, 140–42; Engels on abolition of, 119, 154; as material basis for social inequality, 161–62
proletariat, 52, 98, 129; in advanced capitalist countries, 57; enslaved Blacks as, 87; hereditary, in U.S., 148; private property ended by, 130–31; racial integration of, 166
Putin, Vladimir, 167

race: Hund on, 92–94, 103–6; Louisiana's "one-drop rule" on, 21; Marx and Engels on, 83–100, 124–25; as social construct, 98
racial capitalism, 116, 161, 162
racism, 40, 46; antisemitism and, 107; Hund on, 104; Lenin on,

110; Marx and Engels on, 47, 84; systemic, 152, 153; Trotsky on, 111; Weydemeyer on, 87
Reconstruction, 124; Du Bois on, 145–46; overthrow of, 104–5, 125, 143; Weydemeyer on, 140
Robinson, Cedric, 9, 160–64; in Africa, 27; author's review of *Black Marxism* by, 34–58; on Black Nationalism, 83; on Du Bois, 81; Grenada Revolution omitted by, 161; Hund, Andrew Douglas, and Loggins' reliance on, 115–16; Malcolm X not discussed by, 116–17, 157, 158; on Marxism, 168; on Marx on slavery, 146; on racial capitalism, 161, 162; West on, 7; *see also Black Marxism: The Making of the Black Radical Tradition*
Rodney, Walter, 42
Rogers, Kim Lacy, 18
Rubin, Leslie, 24
Russia, Marx and Engels on, 61, 67, 72–79
Russian Revolution (1917), 76, 78, 111, 167
Russo-Japanese War (1905), 75
Russo-Turkish War (1877), 75

Sankara, Thomas, 12, 163
Scheer, Charlie, 29
Second International (Socialist International), 51, 108, 109
Second Reconstruction, *see* civil rights movement
Second World War, 165
segregation, Supreme Court decisions on, 144
Senate Internal Security Subcommittee, 16–17
sexism, 46
Shabazz, Betty, 114
Sharpeville Massacre (South Africa, 1960), 23–25
1619 Project (New York Times), 120, 141; on failure of Reconstruction, 145; on systematic racism, 152
slave revolts, 50–51, 67; Haitian Revolution as, 99
slavery: Blacks born into, 84–85; capitalism tied to, 45–46; *Capital* on, 138; *Communist Manifesto* on, 131; Frederick Douglass on, 88–90; Marx and Engels on, 85–87, 96, 127–29, 132–33
Social Democracy, 118
socialism, 17; democratic socialism, 154–55; Engels on prospects for, in U.S., 147–48
Socialist Party (U.S,), 109
Socialist Workers Party (SWP): author in, 29–31, 34–36, 59; educational campaign within, 37; James in, 53–55, 112; Malcolm X and, 156–58; Sankara supported by, 163; Trotsky on, 112–14
Sorge, Frederick, 144
South Africa, 23–25, 48, 49, 121
South Africa-Mozambique security pact (Nkomati Accord), 49
Soviet Union: collapse of, 59, 163; CPUSA as apologist for, 166; Trotsky on, 56
Spriggins, E. Belfield, 16, 17, 20, 24
Stalin, Joseph, 56, 111
Stalinism, 53, 56, 166; Trotsky on, 118

Stephens, Alexander, 96, 135
Stevens, Thaddeus, 140–42
Student Nonviolent Coordinating Committee (SNCC), 25–26
Suffrage, *see* voting
Supreme Court (U.S.): *Brown v. Board of Education* decision of, 18–19, 144; *Plessy v. Ferguson* decision of, 105, 144
Syriza Party (Greece), 155
systemic racism, 152, 153

Taiping Rebellion (China), 50, 63
Tanzania, 26–27
Third International (Communist International), 51, 76
Till, Emmett, 17, 22
Tocqueville, Alexis de, 82
Toure, Kwame (Stokely Carmichael), 25
Trotsky, Leon, 30, 53; Douglas and Loggins on, 115; on national question, 54–56; Pathfinder Press' publication of, 114; on racism, 111–14; on Stalinism, 118
Trotskyists, 30, 53
Trump, Donald, 148, 150, 152, 153, 159

Ukraine, 167
Union Army (U.S., Civil War), 90–91, 134
United States, 68; Engels on the prospects for socialism in, 147–48, 158; hereditary working class in, 144–45; northern Mexico captured by, 66; post-Civil War, Engels on, 139–40; as world economic center, 63; *see also* Civil War

voting, 132; in election of 1964, 24; by former slaves, 139–40; Martin Luther King on, 155

West, Cornel, 7, 8, 13, 164
Weydemeyer, Joseph, 84, 141; Engels and, 139; enlists in Union Army, 134; on enslaved Blacks as proletariat, 87; on private property, 142; on suffrage for former slaves, 140; in Union Army, 90–91
whites: Bishop on Black links to, 38; Frederick Douglass on, 138; Du Bois on psychological wage for, 97; expelled from SNCC, 25–26; Marx on, 149; non-slaveholding, in Confederacy, 135–36
white supremacy, 153
Winstanley, Gerard, 130
working class, 32; Black, 149–50; hereditary, in U.S., 144–45
Wright, Daunte, 153
Wright, Richard, 40; in Communist Party, 53

Yamahtta-Taylor, Keeanga, 162
Yates, Michael, 9

Zasulich, Vera, 74, 76
Zimbabwe, 27
Zimmerman, Angela, 84–91